NOT BAD, EH?

Great Moments in Canadian Sports History

Frank Cosentino

GSPH

Published by

GSPH GENERAL STORE
PUBLISHING HOUSE INC.

1 Main Street, Burnstown, Ontario, Canada K0J 1G0
Telephone (613)432-7697   Fax (613)432-7184

ISBN 0-919431-29-1

Printed and bound in Canada.

Designed by Marlene McRoberts, Hugh Malcolm and Bill Slavin

General Store Publishing House Inc. gratefully acknowledges the assistance of the Ontario Arts Council.

An honest attempt has been made to secure permission for the use of all material; if there are errors or omissions, they are wholly unintentional and the author and/or the publisher will be grateful to learn of them.

Measurements: Most of Mr. Cosentino's essays appear in metric measurement; imperial measurement has been retained when it would be more readily understood.

Front Cover Photo: Ethel Catherwood — the Saskatoon Lily, winner of the high-jump gold medal, 1928 Olympics.

Canadian Cataloguing in Publication Data

Cosentino, Frank, 1937 -

    Not bad, eh? : great moments in Canadian sports history

ISBN 0-919431-29-1

    1. Sports — Canada — History.   I. Title.   II. Title: Great moments in Canadian sports history

GV585.C68 1990   796'.0971   C90-090108-X

First Printing November 1990

To my granddaughters:
Sarah Rose, Mary Claire, Nicole Marie
and Danielle Frances

See the conqu'ring hero comes!
Sound the trumpets, beat the drum;
Sports prepare, the laurel bring,
Songs of triumph to him sing.

See the godlike youth advance,
Breathe the flutes, and lead the dance;
Myrtle-wreaths and roses twine,
To deck the hero's brow divine.

See the conqu'ring hero comes!
Sound the trumpets, beat the drums!

From Judas Maccabaeus

by Handel 1685-1759

TABLE OF CONTENTS

Page

"Swim to Canada, Marilyn" — F. Cosentino 11

Marilyn — Toronto Star 23

The Swimmer — Irving Layton 24

Track Meet at Pangnirtung — A.W. Purdy 25

The Swimmer — Arthur Bourinot 26

Canadian Grit! — H. Reginald Hardy 27

George Young . . . Victor — Joseph S. Cook 28

The Matchless Six — F. Cosentino 29

Canadian Women and the Olympic Games — Joesph S. Cook 43

Ottawa's Sweetheart, Canada's Valentine — F. Cosentino 44

Canadian Scene — Patrick Anderson 56

Cricket at the Wicket — Toronto Mail 58

The Marathon of Hope — F. Cosentino 59

In Memoriam — E. Hughes 77

The Decision — E.J. Pratt 78

The Greatest — F. Cosentino 79

Watt's Song — Edmonton Journal 99

Nations May Totter — Edmonton Journal 100

The Grads — Edmonton Journal 101

"Tyger! Tyger! Burning Bright..." — F. Cosentino 102

Canadian Ski Song — Arthur Bourinot 109

The Song of the Ski — Wilson MacDonald 110

Queen of the Hill — Gerry Straatman 113

Slalom Hill — Arthur S. Bourinot 114

Golfers — Irving Layton 115

Lacrosse: The Sport of Canada — Fred Jacob 116

The Loser's Wail — George Phair 118

The Stanley Cup and 1896 — F. Cosentino 119

The Cup Came Back — Globe 129

The MAAA 1902 Stanley Cup Victory — Montreal Star 130

The Goal — Montreal Star 131

Our Seniors Victorious — Tommy 132

Faceoff — ZZZAP 134

When the Bay Freezes — Al Purdy 135

Winter Sketch — ZZZAP 136

Prospecting the Dawson City Way — F. Cosentino 137

Erlebnis — W.J. L'Heureux 144

Howie Morenz Is No More — F. Cosentino 145

Monsieur Joliat — Wilson MacDonald 153

Hail the Conquering Heroes — F. Cosentino 155

Hockey Players — Al Purdy 165

Grey Is The Forelock Now — Joan Finnigan 167

Shut Your Mouth Tourbin — Dennis Tourbin 169

Standing Room Only — Brian Devlin 173

Ned Hanlan — F. Cosentino 174

Edward Hanlan — An Epinikian Ode — W.H.C. Kerr 183

Jacob Gill Gaudaur — Admirer 188

The Race — Lorne Davis 189

How Renforth, N.B., Got Its Name — F. Cosentino 191

The Race, and the Death of James Renforth — B. DeWolfe ... 198

That's Where the West Begins — F. Cosentino 201

Timmis' Exploits — Ted Reeve 210

Grey Cup Fever — Ted Reeve 212

"Swim to Canada, Marilyn"

Perhaps the most famous Canadian during the '50s was a sixteen-year-old Toronto schoolgirl, Marilyn Bell, who captured a nation's heart while performing her heroic swimming feats.

The '50s were difficult times, not only for Canadians but also for the world. On the international scene, a new phrase, "the Cold War," prevailed. Two allies from the second war, the U.S.S.R. and the U.S.A., had drifted apart on a sea of antagonistic idealogies. The "Red Menace," first only a fear, became a reality as a shooting war broke out in Korea. The threat of the atomic bomb lay over us all. When Korea was stabilized, more threats to peace developed in Hungary and the Suez Canal zone. As the Soviet Union asserted itself on the battlefield, so too was it making its mark in sport. It successfully entered the 1952 Olympic Games and the 1954 World Hockey Championships. These successes were followed with the launching of *Sputnik*, the world's first orbiting satellite. It became obvious that the West, and particularly the United States, must endeavour to regain its pre-eminence. After all, it seemed as if American know-how had fallen behind. The Edsel motor car had failed. American

children were deemed to be less fit than European children when measured by the Krause-Webber tests. The Americans were making concerted efforts to regain their position of influence . . . and in doing so, made it doubly difficult for Canadians to develop their Canadian identity. It had always been so by virtue of Canada's position next door to the United States, having the majority of its population along the common border and therefore able to partake of American radio, the new television, music, the movies and its literature.

Indeed, the problem was so acute in Canada that, in 1950, the whole situation was examined by a royal commission which resulted in the *Massey Report*. It stated that the Canadian identity or culture was being submerged in the wake of American influence. It was a problem as old as the country itself. The '50s would provide the impetus for a renewed effort to give greater expression to the concept of Canada. Much of that renewed impetus was to come from Marilyn Bell.

Few people in Toronto, let alone Canada, had ever heard of Marilyn Bell before

September of 1954. Even when she entered and became the first woman to finish the Atlantic City, New Jersey, Marathon Swim on July 18, 1954, her story was missing from most of the country's newspapers. It was only to a small circle of people that Marilyn's name was well-known: to her fellow students at Loretto College where she was a grade-twelve student; to the members of the Lakeshore Swim Club where she had been a member since the age of ten, giving much of her time to the teaching of crippled children; and to her fellow swimmers, and particularly her coach, Gus Ryder, who firmly believed in the innate strength and ability of his young protégée.

Marathon swimming had been a renowned activity on Lake Ontario since the late '20s, particularly in association with the Canadian National Exhibition. Long-distance swimmers, such as George Young, had captured the public's fancy for their much-heralded victories at home and abroad. By the '50s, however, long-distance swimming and the exhibition had declined in popularity among the public. Change was needed. For the 1954 exhibition, efforts were made to stem the decline of its popularity, efforts which seemed to use American talent as the prescription to cure the malady. To head up the grandstand show, American cowboy favourites Dale Evans and Roy Rogers were retained. That in itself was considered to be a major coup. But the exhibition directors gambled that their next announcement would attract even more of the public to the grounds. Florence

Chadwick, the foremost name in American marathon swimming, was commissioned to demonstrate her talent by swimming across Lake Ontario. With great fanfare, it was announced that she would be given ten thousand dollars for her efforts, twenty-five hundred dollars upon entering the water, and the remainder when she successfully crossed the lake.

It appeared that the "Ex" had pulled off a major success. Roy Rogers and Dale Evans, along with Florence Chadwick, were "giants" with all the appeal of the big time and Hollywood. The Ex gleefully encouraged the association. But all did not. On September 3, the yet-unknown Marilyn Bell announced that she would also attempt to conquer Lake Ontario. Marilyn and her coach, Gus Ryder, were indignant that the CNE, in its rush to the United States, had overlooked proven distance swimmers in its own backyard. Marilyn's entry rang out for all to hear. She would attempt to conquer Lake Ontario "for the honour of Canada, for the sake of Canadian swimmers and other athletes, especially for the up-and-coming young ones." Almost immediately, another Canadian swimmer, from St. Thomas, Ontario, Winnie Roach Leuzler, announced that she too would attempt the swim. She was a twenty-eight-year-old distance swimmer, the only Canadian at that time to have conquered the English Channel. A mother of three, her 1951 time for the Channel swim was two minutes slower than Florence Chadwick's.

These developments posed a problem for CNE officials — and Florence Chadwick as

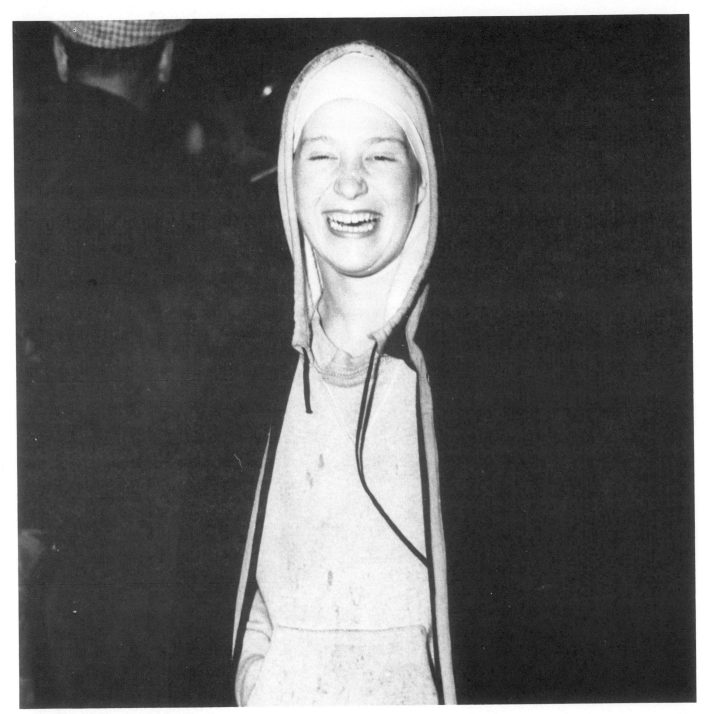

A smiling, refreshed Marilyn.

well. When she had been approached to make the swim, back in May, she had stated her preference to swim alone or not at all. She was to be an attraction, not a competitor. It was too late now for her to back out but she was not at all pleased with the developments which placed her square in the middle of an awkward, nationalistic situation. The CNE sought to save some face while at the same time relishing the extra publicity. Miss Bell and Mrs. Leuzler, they said, were quite welcome to attempt to swim Lake Ontario on their own. The CNE could do nothing about that. But as far as the CNE was concerned, there would not be any prize money for them were they to succeed.

Marilyn was nonplussed. She wasn't in it for the money. Nor did she hold a grudge against Florence Chadwick, she explained. She simply wanted to show what a Canadian could do!

The plucky teen's determination began to capture the hearts of people. Former Toronto controller, Fred Hamilton, announced that he would give five hundred dollars to Marilyn regardless of whether she finished; a Toronto jeweller pledged one thousand dollars. In the midst of all this fanfare an American male, Jerry Woods, declared his intention to enter what was now being described as a race. Suddenly, Lake Ontario was looked upon as one of the great swimming challenges still remaining. Toronto newspapers, radio and television stations began to feature the drama being played out in front of an ever-growing, captive audience.

According to the terms of Florence Chadwick's contract, the crossing had to be finished before the CNE doors closed at midnight, Saturday, September 11. It was estimated that the swim would take some twenty hours; it was scheduled to begin from Youngstown's beach, New York, at 11:00 pm Monday, September 6.

But Monday night, one-and-one-half-metre waves caused the postponement of the fifty-one-kilometre swim. CNE officials left the new starting time up to Florence Chadwick, asking only that a three-hour advance notice be given.

The inclement weather continued all day Tuesday. In *The Globe and Mail*'s words, "no self-respecting walrus" would have chanced the swim. Marilyn slept most of Tuesday as if to gain a reserve of strength. As 11:00 pm neared, she wandered down to the starting area, only to be disappointed once again. Incredulous that the swim could be postponed once more, she waited hopefully until 2:00 am Wednesday before retiring to her motel room once again. It was not only the swimmers who had to be ready for the swim. Each had a supporting cast on hand and on call at all times, ready to lend support and expertise for the long, cold and lonely ordeal. Florence Chadwick, now an uneasy competitor in a race which she never wanted, had an escort boat, the *Anna III*. Aboard were a navigator, doctor, three crew members and two girl-friends. Her coach, Vic Christie, would also accompany her along the swim in a small dory. Marilyn Bell, fast becoming everyone's sentimental favourite, also had an escort boat, the *Mona IV,* carrying a doctor, a nurse, her friend, Jack Russell, *The Toronto Star* reporter, George Bryant, her parents, and her girl-friend, Joan Cooke. Gus Ryder was to follow in a dory, the *Mipepa,* to guide, cajole and inspire as the situation demanded. For Winnie Roach Leuzler, there was only a small dory containing her husband and a doctor. The male swimmer was nowhere to be found.

With each passing hour, tension increased due to the delay. Florence Chadwick was under some pressure to finish the swim before the agreed-to terms of the contract in order to collect her fee. Winnie Roach Leuzler was also under a certain amount of tension since her husband, a member of the RCAF, was being transferred to Calgary on September 13. To Marilyn Bell, it made no difference when the swim began or finished. The worst that could happen was that she might miss a few days of school but for any sixteen-year-old, that was less than calamitous. She was bound to do the swim with or without the sanction of the CNE.

Early Wednesday, September 8, the weather appeared to favour a start. Florence Chadwick decided that she would try once again for an eleven-o'clock start. Immediately, the word spread. The afternoon saw a heavy rainfall and once again the swim was in doubt. By evening, however, the rains had subsided; a calm and placid Lake Ontario followed the storm. All eyes were focused on the Youngstown Yacht Club.

As the starting time approached, flash bulbs began popping. Rival reporters vied with each other to report the events and photograph the surroundings, each one anxious to present a better picture than his competitors. All eyes were on Florence Chadwick as she gently slipped into the cold waters of Lake Ontario. Marilyn was all but ignored, as much a result of her own decision as anything; she chose to allow Florence Chadwick the exposure that was hers because of the arrangement with the CNE. A full minute later, the sixteen-year-old said a little prayer, tucked a four-leaf clover under her bathing cap, gave her mother and father a kiss and a hug, adjusted her swimming goggles and began her journey into the wet darkness. Winnie Roach Leuzler was delayed. Unable to locate her attendants and boat, she was told that they were at the mouth of the Niagara River, some one kilometre from the start. After swimming for about three kilometres and still unable to find them, she withdrew, stating her plan to begin once again in the early morning.

The swim became a nightmare of endurance. Florence Chadwick was showing signs of obvious discomfort as she made her way to the Ontario side of the lake. Ever since her exhibition had turned into a race, she seemed to be showing some signs of strain. She hadn't trained for a race; she wasn't interested in being involved in a contest; she simply wanted to exhibit her swimming prowess on her terms — but now she couldn't do that. Also, the rolling one-metre waves were pitching her about. She became

*A confident
Marilyn enters
the water.*

16

violently ill, six or seven times. She had insisted on continuing but finally, at the insistence of her trainer, she stopped some twenty-four kilometres and six hours into her swim. That very morning she left for California.

Winnie Leuzler, after her night's sleep, entered the water once again just after 6:30 am Thursday morning. The lake began to take its toll of her as well. Severe cramps attacked both of her legs. Still she continued. When it was discovered that her boat did not carry any grease, a signal was sent to land to bring some out. The water was fearfully cold and the grease would act as insulation. To no avail, however. After ten hours and thirty-two kilometres spent in the frigid water, she was forced to withdraw — only moments before a plane dropped some grease for her.

Now only Marilyn was left. She was frightened. The fears of the dark night were magnified as she brushed against fish in the water. Lamprey eels attached themselves to the sixteen-year-old until a frantic kick or slap scurried them on their way. Swimming without grease, she soon removed her ill-fitting goggles as well. As the dawn approached and with it the light, her fears subsided somewhat but now high winds were blowing her off course; the rolling waves were beginning to physically exhaust her. Marilyn felt like quitting. Yet she kept on, stroking mechanically at sixty-five per minute while singing "O Canada" to herself.

By now, a whole city was aware of her progress. Radio stations kept the public informed of her current position and status. Toronto newspapers sought to provide the greatest in-depth coverage ever given a sporting event. The competition among the media, particularly the newspapers, was fierce as each one sought to outdo the others in the scope and magnitude of their stories. By 10:00 am, it appeared as if the swim might end. Her strokes had slowed to fifty per minute. Painful cramps were frequent and severe. By means of a long pole with a cup on the end, she was fed a mixture of corn syrup and Pablum while treading water. Her eyes appealed to Gus Ryder in the boat. Out came a chalkboard on which he wrote various messages: "Fight," or "You can't quit now or you'll let the kids down," or "Flo out of race." A revitalized Marilyn had enough strength to go on, her destination some twenty kilometres off.

By 4:30 in the afternoon, Marilyn was three kilometres away from Toronto. CNE officials were, by now, enthusiastic about the swim. Arrangements were made to set up a light that would flash every thirty seconds and act as a beacon. The water temperature was 10°C. A tense city awaited every item of news surrounding the swim. It was by now being recognized by everyone as a herculean task. Marilyn was slowing down. She stopped swimming four times in five minutes. She would swim for thirty seconds and turn on her back to give her aching muscles a rest and ease the pain. Again she stopped! Ryder's words failed to arouse her! In desperation, he instructed Joan Cooke to jump into the water and swim alongside

Marilyn and offer encouragement. It seemed to be the tonic Marilyn was seeking. When she spotted her friend Joan, in bra and panties, she burst out laughing and began to pick up the pace once again. "Weary Marilyn in sight of CNE. Finds second wind," reported the *Star*.

As word spread throughout the Toronto area, thousands of spectators and well-wishers went down to the lake-shore. All sorts of boats made their way out into the water where the young heroine was struggling towards Toronto. So many, in fact, that she was being impeded. The *Mona IV* radioed the harbour to request assistance in keeping the boats three hundred metres away in order to minimize gasoline residue and increased wave effects.

Marilyn mechanically kept on. With each turn of her head, she saw only "the sky, the waves and the darkness of the water." But if she was mechanical, the public was wound up. The *Telegram* stated:

> *The public was lifted up in a tremendous swell of mass jubilation and thankfulness. Some wept, others cheered. Throughout the rest of the day and into the early evening, every mouth took up the phrase, "How far is she now?" Customers on used-car lots had to wait while salesmen clustered around radios. Truck drivers got used to traffic officers sticking their heads inside cabs with the query: "How far is she now?" Thousands of telephone calls jammed newspaper offices: "How far is she now?"*

Less than three kilometres away from completing the swim, the decision was made to allow Marilyn to drift off course. Her new destination would be to the west, to Sunnyside. One kilogram of corn syrup was fed to her during this last distance. She seemed to be swimming by instinct. Winnie Roach Leuzler, recovering in her motel room, sent a telegram to Marilyn saying simply: "Stay with it!"

Finally, after sixty-three thousand strokes, sixty-four kilometres of swimming and twenty-one hours in the water, Marilyn Bell touched the breakwater, completing the long ordeal. Immediately, hands reached out to help her. She fought them off, thinking that they were pulling her out before the swim had been completed. She was dazed and had obviously completed the swim on instinct.

Thousands, captivated by her superhuman effort, done in their interests, had lined the shore anxious to see this courageous fellow citizen. Boat whistles shrilled in joy as an estimated-quarter-million people stood and craned their necks to see, with teary-eyed pride, this young girl. Seasoned maritimers marvelled at the feat. A taxi driver avowed: "I pulled over to the side of the road and cried two or three times when it looked as if she might not make it. I'll never say women can't do anything in the future."

After a brief respite, Marilyn was taken to the Royal York Hotel for a thorough examination and rest. Canada opened its heart to the young swimmer. Gifts were sent from all over the country. The CNE committed ten thousand dollars to her; another twenty thousand dollars in cash and prizes came from Hamilton; five thousand dollars from the Marilyn Bell Fund; thirty-seven hundred dollars from local business firms; a fund-raising night was held by the Maple Leaf Baseball Club; all in all an estimated two hundred and fifty thousand dollars was contributed to Marilyn Bell. Included among the gifts were an Austin convertible and 1365 litres of gas, an all-expenses-paid holiday and a host of other offerings. The public was anxious to show its appreciation. On Friday evening Marilyn, driving in her new car, was escorted by the RCMP to the CNE. There, before some fifty thousand spectators, Leslie Saunders, the president of the CNE, presented Marilyn with a cheque for ten thousand dollars. The ovation lasted for twenty minutes! When the cheering died down, the Leslie Bell Singers serenaded her with a new composition: "Marilyn." Tears came to the eyes of many, including Marilyn. Escorted to the grandstand, Marilyn was introduced to another huge crowd of twenty-five thousand, by Roy Rogers and Dale Evans, who declared it to be the biggest thrill of their lives. An exhausted but happy Marilyn returned to the Royal York for more rest.

The adoration of the grateful public continued: on Monday, September 13, an estimated one hundred and fifty thousand lined the route from the Royal York to city hall. Ticker-tapes and confetti drifted through the air seemingly held aloft by the cheering throngs. Massed bands played "O

You Beautiful Doll" as the normally staid city opened up its heart to this young patriot. Mayor Leslie Saunders, while presenting Marilyn with a gold, diamond-studded maple leaf, echoed the city's sentiments when he told the teary-eyed conqueror of Lake Ontario: "You have brought honour in the highest degree to this our native land, the Dominion of Canada. Your historic accomplishment has stirred the country from coast to coast and echoes in all corners — in the athletics field and out of it."

Honours and citations of congratulation continued to pour in from all parts of Canada and the United States. Marilyn continued to be front-page news until September 22. Offers from Hollywood, plus the opportunity to appear on the *Ed Sullivan Show* came but Marilyn seemed very anxious to return to her life as a schoolgirl even though the Toronto *Telegram* attempted to place her never-before-done swim into some sort of perspective:

> *Rockets may fly to the moon and atomic energy may turn molehills into mountains but these are victories of minds and machines. The fighting heart of one young girl has brought a thrill and reassurance that no mechanical triumph can quite match.*

For the next ten months, Marilyn directed her energies towards her school work, while maintaining a relaxed swimming schedule of training. To the public, her swimming exploits receded into the background — only to burst on the scene, once again, on July 7,

1955. The Toronto *Telegram* announced that Marilyn was in England, training for an attempt on the English Channel. In a jab at *The Toronto Star* which had had an advantage with the Lake Ontario swim, it gleefully announced at the same time, that it was sponsoring the swim. Daily details would be released in the featured section, "Marilyn's Diary."

For the next month and well into August, Marilyn was once again front-page news. The *Telegram*'s seemingly insatiable readers learned of the events associated with the swim, including Marilyn's visit with the Queen on July 14. On that occasion, she wore a dress representing the Canadian Textile Association. It contained fifty-five metres of nylon and weighed just under threee kilograms! But if the *Telegram* carried an abundance of news, the rival *Star* virtually ignored the event, clearly miffed at the exclusive stories generated by its rival's sponsorship. The stories published in the *Star* seemed to cast doubts upon whether the swim would take place at all. Indeed the swim, scheduled for July 29, was postponed due to high winds. But not for long.

On Saturday, July 30, the *Telegram*'s eight-centimetre headlines declared boldly for all to see: "She goes Sunday." It was an ironic twist since the *Telegram* would not publish until Tuesday, thus giving its rivals an advantage in reporting the swim. The *Telegram* grandly declared: "Nothing must stand in the way of Marilyn's chance to swim the Channel. First chance she gets, off she goes and the best of luck to the girl."

Early during the morning of July 31, Marilyn Bell entered the waters of the English Channel at Cap Gris-Nez, France, bound for the stony shores of the white cliffs of Dover. She was attempting to be the youngest competitor ever to swim across the Channel. Fourteen hours and thirty-six minutes later, at 8:29 pm, she had done it! Tired, her tongue swollen from the salt in the water, she had sprinted the last half-kilometre, increasing her stroke from a low of fifty-eight to seventy-two per minute. She was tired, but pleased. A smile came to her face as one of her entourage handed her a bouquet of purple thistles and Queen Anne's lace. It was another major achievement for the seventeen-year-old.

On her return to Toronto on Friday, August 19, the welcome accorded to her was reported in fifteen-centimetre headlines! Two hundred thousand people turned out in 39°C, temperatures to line the streets for a glimpse of this young girl who once again had stolen their hearts. Above the parade, tonnes of ticker-tape drifted slowly towards the grand sight below. It was a regal reception for a royal accomplishment. Seemingly, Marilyn had topped her Lake Ontario swim with her gritty Channel performance. Were their more worlds to conquer?

There were! Within hours of the completion of the Channel swim, it was announced that in the following year, 1956, Marilyn would attempt to swim the Strait of Juan de Fuca. Some had described it as the Mount Everest of swimming. The channel between Washington State and Vancouver Island was treacherous and had conquered a host of internationally known swimmers, including Florence Chadwick.

On Friday, July 13, 1956, an eighteen-year-old Marilyn Bell left Toronto for Victoria to train for the swim. Some five thousand had come to see her off, presenting her with a horseshoe of flowers. She seemed reserved, almost subdued, talking about the swim in cautious tones. The Strait was far less predictable than the English Channel. The many currents were a mystery even to the many ships' pilots who plied the waters daily. For Marilyn Bell, it would be her greatest challenge.

Once again fifteen-centimetre headlines appeared in the *Telegram* blaring their announcement that Marilyn was beginning her journey. But to those who had watched Marilyn swim previously, she looked different now. Her strokes were shorter, seemingly tighter. Perhaps it was the water temperature, a frigid 9.7°C, or the chilly air temperature, 14°C, which were responsible. Nine hours and fifty minutes into the swim after her 8:46 am beginning, it was obvious that she was struggling. There were only nine kilometres remaining, but Gus Ryder could tell that this wasn't the time to encourage Marilyn to go on. He gave the signal to pull her out of the water. For at least the time being, the Strait had won.

Marilyn seemed more determined than ever to try again. She knew she could do it. Perhaps she had listened too much to those who had extolled the unknown powers of the treacherous waters and had been less than confident about her chances. She knew that the next time would be different. It wasn't the ten thousand dollars that she had lost which upset her — the *Telegram* had offered to pay her that sum if she attempted the swim and another ten thousand dollars on completion. She was determined to prove to herself, more than to anyone else, that she could do it.

And on August 23 she did. As she strode into the water, flashing a victory sign, her coach, Gus Ryder, gave her simple instructions: "Swim to Canada, Marilyn." Her reply was equally assertive: "I will, Gus."

And Marilyn did. Swimming strongly throughout in spite of one-and-one-half-metre waves, Marilyn made the crossing from Port Angeles to Victoria in ten hours and thirty-eight minutes. She was the first Canadian and the first woman to do so. Thirty-five thousand obviously pleased people lined the shore where she landed. Their cheers would be re-echoed for years to come by the erection of a cairn commemorating the swim. For Marilyn, it was to be the last of her major swims. It had been a hectic two years, which began because a sixteen-year-old had wanted to show the world what a Canadian could do, and ended with an eighteen-year-old swimming home to Canada.

Years later, Marilyn has the same wave and smile.

Marilyn

Marilyn, the eyes of the world are on
Marilyn,
The hearts of the world are with
Marilyn,
For we love her so —
Marilyn
We've found a new sweetheart in
Marilyn
For lovelier far is our
Marilyn
Than any girl we know across the Country
wide

A Nation stands in pride
To sing the praise of one who
Came through. It's Marilyn
The Sweetheart of Canada
Marilyn
The toast of the town is our
Marilyn
For we all love her so.

Leslie Bell

Source: The Toronto Star *(11 September 1954), p.25.*

The Swimmer

The afternoon foreclosing, see
The swimmer plunges from his raft,
Opening the spray corollas by his act of war—
The snake heads strike
Quickly and are silent.

Emerging see how for a moment
A brown weed with marvellous bulbs,
He lies imminent upon the water
While light and sound come with a sharp
passion
From the gonad sea around the Poles
And break in bright cockle-shells about his
ears.

He dives, floats, goes under like a thief
Where his blood sings to the tiger shadows
In the scentless greenery that leads him
home,
A male salmon down fretted stairways
Through underwater slums . . .

Stunned by the memory of lost gills
He frames gestures of self-absorption
Upon the skull-like beach;
Observes with instigated eyes
The sun that empties itself upon the water,
And the last wave romping in
To throw its boyhood on the marble sand.

Irving Layton

Track Meet at Pangnirtung

The young Eskimo mothers
line up for a foot race leaving
babies with old women
When the Anglican minister says
                    GO
they gallop like rainbows
a dozen of them
in white parkas with red and blue trim
laughing and panting to the finish line to
reclaim their babies
A white construction worker gives
one old lady a package of cigarettes as
payment for taking her picture so
she smiles a smile from her ancient youth
he takes away with him
            into the leapfrog future
The different age groups of children
line up for sack races
            and piggyback races
                    boy and girl races
and the husbands lounge off to one side

trying to act as if they don't enjoy it
all of them
seahunters from the hungry islands
            now weaponless
No one seems to mind losing here
for losing is a kind of pleasure when
a wounded seal doesn't swim away
            under the ice
            and laughter is
a cold filling between the hours
laughter is
ignorant wisdom of the young
as the old men in their bones
know
            having laughed many times
            with serious faces still
            in the running

A.W. Purdy

Source: North of Summer *(Toronto: McClelland and Stewart).*

The Swimmer

Now these are the joys of the swimmer,
The poise on the brink, then the spring,
The plunge through the air, then the water
That with exultation will fling
Its arms in abandon about him
And coolth of caresses that cling.

Then down with slow strokes to the bottom,
The dim of the depth far below,
The green of the shadowy-water,
The feel of the flesh with its glow,
Swift urge of the strokes to the surface,
The heart with its hammering blow.

Then out with quick strokes of the racer,
The face in the glistening flow,
A rest with the eyes to the heavens
Where argosies splendid and slow

Blow by with slow winds to the sunset,
White frigates of ages ago.

Then back once again to the shore line,
The warmth of the sun on the beach,
The motionless drowse and the dreaming,
The sun with its far-burning reach,
The gossamer haze on the mountains,
The lilt of the water's low speech.

Oh, these are the joys of the swimmer,
The pose on the brink and the glow,
The coolth of the waters around him,
The veins with their maddening flow,
The rush through the arms of the water,
The plunge to the shadows below.

Arthur Bourinot

Canadian Grit!

He did not have a well-filled purse,
*   The backing of the crowd;*
Nor cheering members of a club
*   To shout his name aloud:*
But he had something greater for
*   To send him on his way*
The memory of a mother's face
*   Whose head was streaked with grey.*

He won his fight! The odds were high,
*   And his the high renown,*
The adulation of the world,
*   The victor's laurel crown.*
Beneath the southern skies of blue
*   He held his country's name*
Above the standards of the earth,
*   Playing the British game!*

Throughout the chilling gloom of night
*   He fights the icy sea.*
And keeps his eyes toward the light
*   That urges victory.*
No wave too high, no tide too strong
*   To slow that sturdy crawl.*
Behind him sink the rocky shores,
*   While deeper shadows fall.*

Until in sight of land it seems
*   His dreams cannot come true,*
He keeps his head and sets his lips,
*   And sees the long hours through:*
And now, at last, upon the tides,
*   That cannot help but yield,*
He sweeps towards the longed-for goal
*   To clasp the victor's shield.*

He did not have a giant's frame
*   To span the ice flood;*
A boy with good Canadian grit
*   And valiant Scottish blood;*
And as he battled on and on
*   When other ceased to dare*
Not least of all his simple evils,
*   He had a mother's prayer.*

H. Reginald Hardy

Source: The Toronto Star *(21 January 1927), p.19.*

George Young ... Victor

San Pedro's channel forced at last to yield
To youth's strong arm, and enterprising skill;
Who dared the icy waters, and the field
Of swimmers world renowned, he held at
will.

We won, but back of him a Mother's love
Whose heart throbs in the racing waters
dream
A magic, potent, unseen force did prove,
The loving secret, which dismantled fear.

Such noble triumph with reward well won.
While much to him, to youth at large once
more,
Who find themselves where treacherous
waters run
And battle land to reach a friendly shore.

So with him in his victory we count,
The widowed mother praying for her son;
Whose faith and courage did the waves
surmount,
And earned the highest praise of men, "Well
done."

And in the days of old! twill oft be told
Of how the mem'ry of his mother dear,
With every mile subdued, made him more
bold,
And filled his heart with courage and good
cheer.

Hand we this motto for our youth today:
"I'll not five up till I reach the shore."
A noble purpose adding strength and stay
Till "Victory" met him at her open door.

A hero now, a hero let him be,
When nature shall again take her place;
For subtle ties are running in life's sea,
But grit like his shall win the greater race.

Joseph S. Cook

Source: The Globe and Mail (22 January
1927).

28

The Matchless Six

If ever an institution was considered to be a bastion of male dominance, it was the ancient Olympic Games. In those early contests, women competitors were not only barred, they were prohibited by pain of death from even watching! It was only natural, thought founder Pierre de Coubertin, that when the Olympics were revived in 1896, they too would be for males only.

Eventually, there came to be exceptions. As early as 1908, women were allowed to compete in tennis and swimming but it wasn't until 1928, at the Amsterdam Olympics, that women's track and field events were included for the first time. It was not a unanimous decision — far from it. To many it seemed to be far ahead of its time. In many countries, women did not even have a vote in elections. In Canada, for example, it was only in 1917 that women were enfranchised for federal elections. Indeed there was such a furore about the inclusion of such a strenuous activity as track and field for females that the Olympic Committee was split and a special meeting had to be called to discuss it. It was only narrowly approved despite strong objections from countries such as Canada and the Vatican. Their objections, and those of others similarly inclined, were based upon the popular opinion that women were too frail to be involved in such activities, particularly the 800-metre run.

Nonetheless, with the decision made to include women's track and field events, Canada set a process in motion to select its representative team. Various regions held meets and the winners would attend the Dominion Trials in Halifax where Canada's first female Olympic team would be selected. Six women were chosen; six who had made names for themselves in the thriving world of women's sport in the '20s in Canada.

Myrtle Cook, twenty-six, from Toronto, had only recently set an international indoor sprint record at a meet in New York. At the trials in Halifax, she ran the 100 metres in twelve seconds. She would represent Canada in the 100 metres and the 400-metre relay.

Ethel Smith, a twenty-year-old from Toronto, would also enter the 100-metre run and the 400-metre relay. She was well-known in the Toronto area as a softball and basketball player.

Bobbie "Fanny" Rosenfeld was an outstanding all-around athlete. She was born in Russia in 1905 but had moved to Toronto at an early age, and became a citizen of Canada in 1920. She was prominent in sports such as softball and basketball in addition to track and field. She held Canadian records in the long jump, standing long jump, discus and shot-put. So prominent was Bobbie Rosenfeld in Canadian sport that she would be selected, in 1950, as Canada's outstanding female athlete of the first half-century. Bobbie was set to enter the 800-metre and 100-metre runs, the discus and the 400-metre relay.

Ethel Catherwood, a nineteen-year-old, was born in Hannah, North Dakota, and she too had moved to Canada at an early age, settling in Saskatoon. She was a striking beauty as well as a very hard-working athlete. Some said that she was the most photographed girl at the games, with athletes and photographers alike wanting to capture the radiance and beauty of the woman dubbed the Saskatoon Lily. She held the Canadian high-jump record and had equalled the world record of 1.6 metres at the trials in Halifax. She would represent Canada in her specialty.

Jean Thompson was only seventeen. She was also known as the Penetanguishene Pansy, a name inspired by the town where she was also known as an outstanding softball pitcher. At the Canadian National Exhibition games, she had won the under-eighteen 100-metre race. She would compete in that as well as the 800-metre race.

The sixth member of the team was another eighteen-year-old, Florence Bell. She, too, was a versatile performer excelling in hurdling as well as swimming and softball.

With the trials complete and the team selected, some important decisions were necessary. For Ethel Smith and Myrtle Cook, it was necessary to postpone planned weddings in order to represent Canada. It was a much-saluted decision. The girls were described as having a fine sense of sportsmanship while their husbands-to-be were said to have the patience of Job for their concurrence. There was no question in the minds of all that this was a serious venture. The six were asked to sign the following pledge:

> *In the event of my being selected on the Canadian women's Olympic team, I solemnly promise that I will go to Europe with the team and that I unconditionally obey both the chaperon and manager until my return to Canada. Also that I will put myself in the hands of the Canadian coach only and that I will at all times conduct myself so as to uphold the honour of Canada. The penalty for breaking the above pledge is forfeiture of my place on the team.*

However, no decisions were needed when it came to travelling outfits. They were all provided. They consisted of white silk blouses, white pleated flannel skirts, white silk stockings, scarlet shoes, a red hat and a white blazer with red piping, and a maple leaf crest. Nor were there too many decisions to be made about what to do during any spare

Myrtle Cook was disqualified in the 100m race of the 1928 Olympics after two false starts.

time on board the ship during the ten-day ocean voyage. Manager M.M. Robinson informed all team members, men and women, that they would be treated alike in terms of diet and the following team regimen:

8:00 am - Swim
9:00 am - Breakfast
10:30 am- 12:00 noon - Gymnasium
   work-out
1.00 pm - Lunch
2:30 pm- 3:30 pm - Walk
3:30 pm - Deck games
6:00 pm - Supper
10:00 pm - Bed
 10:30 pm - Visit from Manager and
   Chaperon
Lights Out

On July 20, the team arrived in Amsterdam. From the day they left Union Station in Toronto for the trip to Montreal, there was little fanfare surrounding the women's team. But, if there was a hush at home, there was excitement in Holland. The controversy surrounding the women's events swirled even as Queen Wilhelmena of the Netherlands pronounced the games open. At the opening ceremonies, the Canadian women marched behind a flag which had been carried previously by the victorious 1924 hockey team. They caused quite a ripple of excitement, but not nearly as much as when they appeared in their running outfits. Their shorts were somewhat briefer than others', while the sleeves of their shirts were cut out in order to give more freedom of movement to the arms.

The 1928 games represent a peak in Canadian Olympic history. The sporting world was shocked when Canada's Percy Williams was proclaimed the world's fastest human being, winning the 100-metre and 200-metre gold medals. The men's team also won silver medals in the 400-metre race — James Ball, middleweight wrestling — D. Stockton, double sculls — Jack Guest, Joe Wright and bronzes in the 1600-metre relay, bantamweight wrestling — Jim Trifunov, welterweight wrestling —Maurice Letchford, the argonaut rowing eights and the 800-metre relay swim. It was a much-welcome performance after the 1924 Games but it remained for the newly formed women's team to provide yet another wave of euphoria.

Perhaps some indication of what was to come should have been gleaned from the women's 100-metre heats. Ethel Smith caused a great sensation when she defeated the reigning North American champion, Rosa O'Neill, and thereby qualified. She joined Fanny Rosenfeld and Myrtle Cook in the gold-medal race along with two Germans and an American.

In the ancient Olympics those who anticipated the start, and broke before the starter's signal, were flogged. (A situation which evoked a comment from a sage observer that those who do not anticipate are left at the start.) At the 1928 games, perhaps Myrtle Cook and a German competitor would have preferred the ancient punishment. Each of them had two false starts . . . and both were disqualified. Myrtle Cook's heart was broken. She was the only one of the six with international experience. Much was expected of her and she had been determined to give her all in order to win the gold. She had deliberately prepared her starting holes in the cinder track. This was to be the culmination of all of her efforts and hard work. Now she was in a daze, the

4 x 100m Gold Medal team, 1928 Olympics: Florence Bell, Myrtle Cook, Ethel Smith, Bobbie Rosenfeld..

sadness too heavy to be real. She slowly made her way to the middle of the infield, unable to stem the flow of tears for the next half-hour.

Back at the starting line, only four competitors remained. Fanny Rosenfeld and Ethel Smith reminded each other to await the starter's gun.

At the crack of the pistol, a roar came from the crowd as if in echo to the shot. Twelve and two-tenths seconds later, the two Canadians and the American hit the tape seemingly at the same time. Jubilation reigned in the Canadian camp; they were sure that Fanny Rosenfeld had come first. But when the official results were posted, after much deliberation, Fanny was second and Ethel Smith was third. Each was given the same time as the winner, Elizabeth Robinson of the United States. The Canadians launched an official protest but to no avail — the Canadian Amateur Athletic Union president, Dr. Lamb, refused to back the appeal, thus ensuring its defeat. All attempts to reschedule the race, even as an informal world championship, were also turned down. Criticism of the American starter, John Taylor of Chicago, was so intense and persistent that he resigned from the Olympic staff.

To their credit, the women's team put their disappointment behind them, accepted the fact that they had won the silver and bronze but not the gold and prepared for the next event. Jean Thompson, the Penetanguishene Pansy, shocked the games when she came

first and set a new world record in the 800-metre heat. Her time was 2:31:5 but the record lasted only one day. A German competitor set a new one with a winning time of 2:16:5. The still-learning Jean Thompson was fourth, Bobbie Rosenfeld, fifth. Now Canada's hopes rested on five athletes and two events, the quartet of Fanny Rosenfeld, Ethel Smith, Florence Bell and Myrtle Cook, and Ethel Catherwood in the high jump.

First came the 400-metre relay. Each competitor would run one hundred metres. All four wanted desperately to run their best time in this meet against the best. Three of them wanted to prove to all that they should have won the gold in the 100-metre dash. Each of the four placed herself at the appropriate interval around the oval. Fanny Rosenfeld took her place at the start. The athlete who was invariably described as the life of the party was now very serious. The chocolate factory worker was now a study in determination as she carried the special baton presented to the team by the Hamilton Olympic Club. She walked to the footholds she had carefully dug out of the cinder track. It was a good track. Where none had expected the setting of any new records, a total of seventeen in the twenty-seven events held were set. Fanny already had a silver in the 100 metres and a fifth in the 800 metres, a feat which in itself demonstrated the great depth of her talent. She also had broken the existing record in the 800 metres while placing fifth, no mean accomplishment for an athlete who was considered a sprinter. She might have even won, or come close enough to pick up some points for her team, had she decided to enter the discus event but there was only enough time to do a certain number of things if she wanted to do them well. At the Halifax trials, she had tossed it 39.345 metres. The winning effort at Amsterdam was 39.624 metres. But she couldn't do everything. It was decided that she should save some of her strength for the 400-metre relay and now, it was here.

Bobbie "Fanny" Rosenfeld, Canada's Female Athlete of the First Fifty Years.

As her hands and feet strained against the cinders, her eyes set, looking straight ahead, her ears tuned to the smallest sound, Fanny broke from the starting line a split-second before the gun. Another shot rang out. The runners were recalled; Fanny was warned. One more false start meant disqualification not only for her but for the whole team. Knowing looks were exchanged by all the Canadian team members, their eyes meeting over the 400-metre track. No words were necessary since the memory of the 100 metres was still fresh in everybody's minds. For Bobbie "Fanny" Rosenfeld, the solution was obvious: she must stay fixed in her starter's stance until she heard the report of the gun — no matter what. It might mean a split-second, couple-of-steps disadvantage, but there was no other way.

When the starter's pistol rang out, Fanny was a full step behind the others. It was disconcerting because the first forty metres were the most important since it was in that space that an athlete used her strength and power to move from a full stop to high speed. Now she was two steps behind. By sheer determination, she closed the gap as she moved towards the exchange area. When she handed the baton to Ethel Smith, she had narrowed the gap to one step. The exchange was smooth. It had been practised countless times not only in Amsterdam and in Canada but also aboard the *Albertic* during the two-week voyage. Fanny continued running at full speed a full second or so after the exchange before slowing down, her gaze fixed on the progress of the race. Ethel Smith,

meanwhile, had only one thing on her mind and that was to run as fast as she could to make up the distance she was behind. The baton seemed to have so much importance, and yet it was probable that the feelings the athletes had for each other, from the constant months of association with one another, were responsible for the strain and effort that each was demanding of herself. Ethel Smith held her eyes on the space beyond the leader as she hurtled down the track hoping to close the distance in the short space of one hundred metres. She passed a competitor! Now the baton was given to Florence Bell.

Like the others, Florence, too, had something to prove. Her previous race, the heat of the 100 metres, was her first international exposure. She knew, and so did the others, that she simply had a case of the jitters. She was overcome by the awesomeness of the games. She had been used to competing in small, quiet and reserved meets before a handful of spectators. All had told her about the crowd noise, the media, the tremendous amount of traffic of athletes around the grounds, but to hear of it and to experience it were two different things. She was just pleased that she had another chance to learn from her experience. Her elimination in the first heat was unique among her team-mates. She was determined that she would give a good account of herself today. More ground was made up as Florence leaned into the turn and aimed herself down the straightaway. Now she was in the middle of the pack. Both she and Myrtle Cook had to concentrate on the

Ethel Catherwood — the most-photographed girl at the games.

37

exchange; Myrtle would be launched on the last leg in the quest for the gold.

For Myrtle Cook, it must have seemed like a reprieve. Disqualified in the 100 metres, she had to forget her bitter experience and disappointment and prove to herself, and the world, that she was the fastest. She cherished the thought of a second chance at a gold medal but she did not relish the distinct possibility that the race might be decided before the baton arrived. In a semi-crouch, she had followed the progress of her team-mates around the track, straightening up only when she saw the perfect exchange between Ethel and Florence. Now she waited until it was time to begin her sprint in the hand-off area. All of the planning and preparation of months past had come down to one hundred metres and twelve seconds.

When the baton slapped into her tiny hand, Myrtle Cook drove her legs like pistons, keeping her feet close to the ground while stretching out towards the finish line. With seventy-five metres to go, she had pulled even with the leaders. With fifty, she had edged ahead. At the finish, she was several strides ahead! In a dazzling display, the Canadian women had yet another world record with a time of 49:4. It was also the fourth gold medal of the games for the Canadian team.

Whether it was the fact that the women's team had won the gold medal or had a good chance at the team championships or that they all had come through with the best performance in the world, whatever the reason, there was pure, unrestrained joy among them as they all converged on the joyously exhausted Myrtle Cook. They were happiness personified. They alternately hugged and patted each other, whooped and cheered, laughed and cried as their emotions ran through the full gamut of expression. First they would have their celebration, then they would cheer Ethel Catherwood on in her quest for the high-jump title.

Ethel Catherwood had a certain calm about her. She seemed to convey a quiet sort of confidence, an aura of tranquillity, even when she qualified a distant seventeenth for the Olympic finals. In some ways, she was disappointed that one of her favourite sports, the javelin, was not among those included in the games. She was almost as accomplished in that as she was in the high jump. As a matter of fact, she held the Canadian record of 36.17 metres. But she had put all of that behind her. It was time now to concentrate on the high jump.

The bar began at the height of 1.37 metres. Ethel kept her sweat-suit on. She decided to keep it on until the bar was raised to the 1.5-metre level where she jumped, still with it on, and missed! Now it was time to get serious. At the last moment, immediately prior to her second jump, off came the suit. The bar was cleared. Slowly, the bar was moved above 1.5 metres. One by one, the competitors dropped off, unable to negotiate the jump. Ethel was jumping with her determined confidence now, clearing the bar at every height. At the 1.6-metre mark, a new world record, there were three competitors

Ethel Catherwood — the Saskatoon Lily, winner of the high-jump gold medal, 1928 Olympics.

remaining. Catherwood of Canada, Gisolf of Holland who was, naturally, the local favourite, and the international favourite, Mildred Wiley of the United States. The concentration of all three was intense. No Brill Bends or Western Rolls here. It was straight power jumping, the modified scissors style the preferred jump. Each movement would have to be perfectly co-ordinated, almost choreographed, and executed. Not only was the jump something to overcome, there was also the distraction of the Amsterdam crowd, naturally, cheering for its own. Ethel Catherwood would need all of her studied calm now to block everything out of her mind and think only of the jump. Hers was the first jump. She was tired. The competition had taken three hours to this point. It would be over soon which in itself could help to break one's concentration just when more was needed. One miss could mean the end. This was her tenth jump. Her legs were aching. Hanging in the balance was not only a gold medal but the team championship as well. But all of that had to be removed from her mind. Only the bar at 1.6 metres could matter to her now!

With deliberate, measured steps she would have to ease into her approach but first, for what seemed the longest time, Ethel stood back from the bar sorting out and dismissing all of her fears until only the vision of the bar remained with her. Now she was approaching the bar in her practised manner. At the precise launching point which her mind had predetermined, Ethel Catherwood launched herself from her right foot and into the air

above and toward the bar, her left leg rising as if to meet the air at a point already known. At that instant, down came the left, followed by the stiffened right. Ethel fell to the sand-pit and listened for the crowd to confirm what seemed a successful jump. She looked up. The bar was still in place. A feeling of relief came over her as she dusted the sand from her body. It was amazing how many times she had landed in the sand-pit and not felt any pain until after the competition when every bump and bruise seemed intent on reminding her of each landing. She made her way over to the competitors' area, there to watch her opponents' jumps and prepare herself for the next one.

It wasn't necessary. Both the Dutch and the American athletes were unable to handle the jump successfully. Ethel Catherwood had won the gold medal! The Matchless Six had won the Olympic championship! Ethel's team-mates poured from the stands to congratulate her. Jubilation reigned supreme as they all rushed towards the Saskatoon Lily. It was a happy and ecstatic young lady who was hoisted above the shoulders of her Canadian team-mates and paraded before the large and admiring throng. The calm and tranquillity had left her face now, replaced by a beaming, celebrated smile. Ethel's jump had clinched the championship; there weren't any judges or arbitration boards that could take that away from them!

After the closing ceremonies, the women's team began to prepare for home. In the meantime, the Olympic committee would

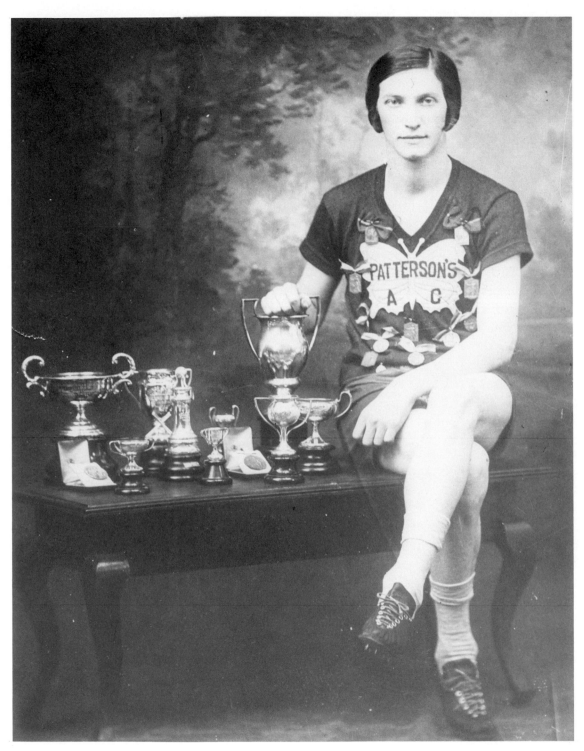

Bobbie Rosenfeld, a one-woman team for Patterson's chocolates.

review the women's track and field performance and decide its future fate. On August 6, a vote was taken. By a sixteen-to-six margin, the track and field program for women was retained but, strangely enough, the Canadian delegation voted against its retention. There was still a widely held feeling that it was too strenuous for women, and, as a concession to that view, the program was trimmed of its more demanding sports. Dropped were the 800-metre run, the long jump, the shot-put and the 200-metre run. Included were the less strenuous 100-metre run, 400-metre relay, the high jump, discus, javelin and the 80-metre hurdles. When one realizes that the marathon was approved for the 1984 games, the 1928 decision seems ludicrous but the experts of the time condoned the widespread support of the theory that any run longer than one hundred metres was too strenuous for female athletes.

On August 26, the triumphant women's team arrived in Canada, their return delayed by appearances in England and France. Their welcome home was an occasion for delirium in each place they stopped. At Montreal they toured an admiring city. Silver compacts and civic banquets were the order of the day. In Toronto, an estimated two hundred thousand people jammed Union Station, overflowing along Front Street and hanging from the windows of the Royal York Hotel. The six kilometres along the parade route to Sunnyside were undertaken after the city of Toronto presented each of the Matchless Six with gold watches and silver cases. Along the route to Sunnyside, another one hundred thousand came to pay their homage.

At Sunnyside, a platform was erected for the darlings of the public. Each was introduced from the platform where presentations of silver tea-services were made, the crowd breaking out into a spontaneous rendition of "See Them Smiling Just Now." In Hamilton, where a special reception was held, medals were awarded in grateful appreciation. A group of Toronto businessmen presented Fanny Rosenfeld with a new car; everywhere, the girls were cheered and honoured by a grateful public. Meanwhile, Ethel Catherwood was making her way home to Saskatoon where there was more excitement than at the end of the First World War. More than two thousand were jammed into the train station when the Saskatoon Lily arrived. There had never been anything like it. The Bedford Road Collegiate student body from Ethel's former high school provided a guard of honour while local dignitaries sang her praises. A three-thousand-dollar educational fund was created for her, a gift she cherished since it would allow her to continue to study the piano.

It was 1928. Some dubbed it the Aspirin Age: the golden age of women's sport. And Canada's Matchless Six were at the top of the world.

Canadian Women and the Olympic Games

Not so our men alone shall praise be given,
For deeds transcending those with whom
they've striven
In the Olympic trials of the world,
Where they conspicuously their flag unfurled.
But for our women equally we claim
To have upheld fair Canada's great name;
For they surpassed in field and track and
score
Their rivals gather from the wide world o'er.

And while for Canada our hearts are
thrilled,
For her high hopes have greatly been
fulfilled;
Toronto, as the home of those who won,
Elated is with joy at what they've done,
Their great achievement will reflected be
In college, home and school from sea to sea:
Let then the winds our thanks sincere
convey,
Hopes, they have brightened for the coming
day.

The equal of her brother she has proved
Her worth, and holds her solid place
unmoved
In letters, art, and every kind of lore,
And calmly waits new kingdoms to explore;
In mental fitness she has well excelled,
And now a record makes in track and field;
Proving her mettle for the stronger role,
Where man had thought he had complete
control.

Nor is her present vict'ry a surprise
To those who live today with open eyes;
Her progress in the varied fields of sport
Is to the good, though dearly it be bought;
The price of excellence is sacrifice,
And those alone who offer reach the prize;
This message of the Olympiad —
"None here may enter till the price is paid;
And what is true of the Olympic strife
Is true of every phase of human life."

Joseph S. Cook

Ottawa's Sweetheart, Canada's Valentine

"Dear Barbara Ann: Your public would
Prefer to show its gratitude
With tributes rare and wonderful
And, preferably tangible.
A rope of pearls, a wrap of mink,
A private indoor skating rink,
A larger Buick, still and creamier
With testimonials from the Premier.
But since such gifts are out of line,
We send this simple Valentine —
A licence, issued to your art
To skate school figures on our heart."

Mary Lowry Ross, "Dear Barbara Ann", *Saturday Night* (14 February 1948).

It's doubtful whether the Canadian nation has ever had a love affair to compare with its one with Barbara Ann Scott in the late '40s. Prime Ministers, premiers, mayors and citizens from all walks of life from coast to coast were captivated by this young, charming nineteen-year-old. Prime Minister Mackenzie King, at a civic luncheon in her honour, opined:

Canada herself takes you into her heart today. You have brought great honour and distinction, not only to yourself but to your country as a whole. From one end of Canada to the other, more people have followed your travels and your contests than was ever the case before . . .
In the days when the clouds have been gathering all around us, you have shone forth like a bright star in a troubled world. Your star has given us courage and strength to help us through the gloom. Thank you for the excellent service you have performed.

Why? What great feat had this young lady performed to give Canadians the "courage and strength" to let them see "through the gloom?"

The Canada of the late '40s should have been a happy one. After all, the Second World War was over in 1945; the troops had come home and all looked forward to normalcy resuming. It was not to be. The Soviet Union and its former allies, Canada included, became suspicious of one another. A cold war enveloped the world which now was treading lightly under the threat of the atomic bomb. Dramatically, Canada was thrust into the middle of the "freeze" when a Soviet cipher clerk, Igor Gouzenko, defected

44

to Ottawa, seeking political asylum in Canada. With him, he carried details of a huge, Soviet espionage ring. Now the tensions in eastern Europe, and Germany were closely identified with those in Canada. Day by day reports did, indeed, tend to be gloomy. Yet, as life moved on, the smiling efforts of a tiny princess were as a beacon of light dispersing any and all thoughts of gloom.

Barbara Ann Scott was born May 9, 1929, to Mary and Clyde Scott, in Ottawa. Her father was an invalid, having been wounded and left for dead before being found and taken as a prisoner of war in April 1915. On his return to Ottawa, the proud lieutenant married. Although rated seventy-five per cent incapacitated, by the army, he sought to live a full life, enjoying a game of golf whenever possible. Barbara Ann was obviously a joy to the Scotts. Her childhood was a happy one, spent with her pets (a Pekingese and Scottie dog, an angora cat, a canary, two rabbits, mud turtles and white mice) and occasionally acting as caddie for her father's golf game.

She loved all sports, especially swimming, golf, and horseback riding, each one vying for her time with the piano. At six, she was given a pair of skates. But it was a while before she could use them. Confined to bed with mastoid problems, she proudly wore her treasured skates anyway. Eventually, the problem was corrected and Barbara Ann settled into a routine of rising at 6:00 am to practise the piano for one and a half hours, have breakfast, go to school,then skate in the afternoon at the Minto Club where she soon won a part as Raggedy Ann in the club's carnival.

She obviously had talent but too many activities were competing for her time. Something had to go. After much deliberation, it was decided to take her out of school and educate her at home with the help of a tutor. Barbara Ann's part of the agreement was that she would continue to practise the piano faithfully and remain near the top of her grade. She thrived! Her bronze skating test was passed at eight, the silver when she was nine and the gold at ten. At ten, she entered the Canadian junior ladies' championships in Toronto. It was her first real exposure to this form of competition. The tiny pixie had to wrap gauze around her ankles in order to have her skates fit tightly but she was an absolute delight to all as she placed fifth.

Under the tutelage of Otto Gold of Czechoslovakia, who arrived at the Minto Club in 1939, Barbara Ann continued to improve. The Scott family, making do on a three-thousand-dollar pension, gave all of the assistance they could. The next year, in 1940, Barbara Ann won the Canadian junior ladies' championship in Ottawa. She continued her brilliant development by placing second in the seniors. She was asked to represent Canada at the North American championships in Philadelphia. It was not a good experience for the youngster; she suffered from dizzy spells and high fever. Some thought it was only from the tension of such a high level of competition. Barbara Ann still came in fifth — creditable, but below her expectations. Everything seemed to be explained when it was discovered that she had the measles!

In 1942, when she was thirteen, Barbara Ann's father died. All of the burden of bringing her up shifted to her mother, who, fortunately, was indeed a strong-willed person. Encouragement and support were offered to the youngster who, by now, was attracting international attention and acclaim. By the time she was fifteen, she won the Canadian seniors; at sixteen and seventeen she won consecutive North American titles. As if to signal that a new era had begun, coincident with the end of the war, Barbara Ann Scott had attracted such attention at home that she was named winner of the 1945 Lou Marsh Trophy. More significantly, it was the first time that the trophy, given annually to Canada's outstanding athlete of the year, was ever won by a woman.

But if Barbara was attracting such attention at home, 1947 was the year that she was acclaimed across the Atlantic. The European and world championships were being held that year, in Switzerland and Sweden respectively. While all in Canada agreed that it would be good for Barbara Ann to enter, there was also the recognition that her mother could not afford to send her daughter throughout the world to compete. Clyde Scott's friends came to the rescue and preparations were made to send the young hopeful to Europe — along with her new coach, Sheldon Galbreath.

There were some who cautioned against asking too much from Barbara Ann. After all, the European championships would be held out of doors and were therefore subject to weather conditions previously unknown to the young Ottawan. It was not unknown to have high winds, glaring sun or melting ice at such events. The artificial indoor arenas which existed in North America were not to be found in Europe. In addition, a hockey tournament was usually held at the same time, a factor which could cause ice ruts and unevenness in the ice surface. There were also those who felt that Barbara Ann should have stayed in Canada to defend her championship indoors and then leave for the world title meet with guaranteed good impressions in everyone's mind.

But Barbara Ann's mind was made up. She wanted to be in Switzerland for the European title and in Sweden for the world title and she was determined to do so! On February 1, 1947, the young skater from Ottawa, after a scintillating performance, was proclaimed champion of Europe at the competitions in Davos, Switzerland. Much was made of the fact that she was the seventh to skate, was given a bouquet of seven roses by the manager of the Belvedere Hotel where Barbara Ann stayed, and was sent a card decorated with seven silver stars. She also wore her coach's tie-pin for extra luck. But it was also obvious that she had no need for any superstitions. Her skating was enough. She sparkled in her performance and clearly demonstrated that she was the best figure skater in the competition.

Almost immediately, she left by air for Stockholm and the world championships. She was confident. After all, the best skaters in Europe had been in Davos and she had previously shown herself to be the best in North America. Nonetheless, the eighteen-year-old was unwilling to leave anything to chance. Every opportunity was spent refining her performance. She polished and practised and polished. At the end of the compulsory school figures, she was ahead, having gained firsts in each. Her performance

Barbara Ann Scott, Canada's sweetheart.

was all the more remarkable because of the extreme cold and the biting wind, both ignored by virtue of Barbara Ann's intense concentration. When the results of the free-skating competition were posted and Barbara Ann declared the winner, the exuberant spectators who had taken this remarkably beautiful doll to their hearts, swarmed over the barriers to congratulate her. Two sixes, perfect scores, were among the marks awarded by the eight judges who placed her first. The young Ottawa miss was given a gold medal and bracelet: she was world champion. Now fifteen thousand Swedes exploded with obvious delight as the president of Sweden presented her with a bouquet of flowers. In a very tender scene, Barbara Ann kept one for herself and presented the rest to her mother.

While congratulatory messages poured in from all around the world, the newly crowned queen made her way to Paris, where, before an adoring throng of twenty thousand mesmerized by her artistry, she skated an exhibition and was presented with the French Medal of Champions, the first woman to receive it. Across the Channel in London, yet another exhibition in Wembley Stadium was similarly enchanting. It was Barbara Ann's last appearance in 1947. Canada's Ice Queen left for home aboard the liner *Queen Elizabeth*.

In Ottawa, preparations were in progress for a huge welcome. School children were given a half-day holiday and thousands turned out to see the city's favourite daughter. Police and firemen provided a guard of honour while the Governor General's Foot Guards Band played "Hail the Conquering Hero" along with a rousing rendition of "Let Me Call You Sweetheart." At the civic luncheon, Mayor Stanley Lewis, speaking for all of his fellow citizens, said: "This occasion is to welcome you and to pay tribute to your genius, your achievement and the charming qualities that make you the world figure skating champion of 1947, a loved as well as an honoured citizen of this capital." With that, he presented her with the keys to a shiny yellow Buick, the licence number a self-explaining 47 U 1.

The gift created a furore in amateur circles. Immediately, Avery Brundage, President of the International Olympic Committee, ruled that the gift contravened the rules of amateurism. Barbara Ann would have to return the gift or forfeit the opportunity to compete in the 1948 world and Olympic competitions. Furthermore, Brundage pronounced, if Barbara Ann accepted either any jewellery or the movie contract which she had been offered, the same censure would apply. The Ottawan and Canadian publics were infuriated. It seemed to be a deliberate attempt to quell their desire to show their gratitude. For Barbara Ann, there was only one thing to do. The answer was obvious. She had not received any jewellery, was not going to accept the offer to go to Hollywood and she would return the car. "It would be selfish of me to keep the car and lose a chance to bring honour to Canada in the Olympics," she explained. With all of the controversy still swirling about, she quietly prepared for

Barbara Ann Scott, Olympic Gold Medallist 1948.

the North American championships to he held in late March. In a sport where traditionally only a few points separate the first and second places, Barbara Ann was 164.1 points better than the runner-up.

One would have thought that Barbara Ann would have had an easy and relaxing summer, that year in 1947. But the heavy competitions of 1948, the Europeans, the worlds and the Olympics, fourteen weeks in all in Europe, were always on her mind. While temperatures in Ontario soared into the thirties, Barbara Ann Scott made her way to the small northern Ontario community of Schumacher where, for nine hours each day, six days each week, she tried to perfect her almost flawless skating, indoors on the artificial ice. The cool northern evenings managed to maintain the hardness of the ice into the middle of the sweltering days but still, some were sceptical about her regimen. The training was all indoors, they repeated once again, isolated from the hostile outdoor reality of the European rinks. Nonetheless the controversy swirled above Barbara Ann; she continued to hone her skills.

By now, the crusade of the world champion was attracting a groundswell of support. In late November 1947, Mayor Lewis of Ottawa announced the creation of a fund to send the city's favourite citizen to Europe. Almost immediately, there was a willing response from across the country. Seven thousand dollars was the goal; it was easily reached. Cheques continued to arrive even after the skater and her entourage prepared to leave.

On December 16, 1947, Barbara Ann, her mother, and coach Sheldon Galbreath, left for England en route to Switzerland. Fresh in her memory were the receptions given to her by the Minto Club, with the presentation of the maple leaf which she said she would wear, and by the government, which through the Hon. Paul Martin, presented her with the National Amateur Athletic Achievement Award. Many accolades were paid to Barbara Ann by officials, politicians, the public and the Governor General. But the one which stayed with her the longest was an "Open Letter to the Champion" printed in *The Ottawa Citizen* December 13, 1947:

> *Dear Barbara Ann:*
> *Tomorrow you set out once again in quest of further skating Laurels. This time, it is for the greatest prize of all — the Olympic Crown in the realm of women's figure skating in which for almost a year now you have reigned supreme. As the plane which bears you on the first stage of this momentous journey to Switzerland takes off, you who have worked so long and so diligently for this trial of skill and courage against the world's best, will know, without our telling you it that you carry with you our heartfelt hopes for success of every Ottawan, every Canadian.*
> *Looking back, it seems no time at all since you returned to us in a blaze of international glory, bringing with you two great honours in the wake of the North American championships you won two years ago.*

Cables flashed the news about the globe that a new and brilliant star had appeared on the athletic firmament. Newsmen vied to pick words adequate to describe the beauty and poise of flawless performances, the fresh loveliness of the performer. Applause was showered on you in Prague, Paris, London and New York; congratulations poured in from the highly placed and the lowly of the two continents.

Yet, you kept your head Barbara Ann! Back home again, undeterred by other's clashes over canary-coloured cars and movie contracts, you stuck to your arduous training with the determination you have shown since childhood. The will to work. The will to win. Ottawa is proud of you, Barbara Ann! In those minutes of great endeavour on Switzerland ice a few short weeks hence, Ottawa's heart will be with you. Goodbye and God speed, Barbara Ann, the very best of luck.

Since two of the competitions in Europe were to be in Switzerland, it was decided to make Davos home base. It was a somewhat familiar surrounding to Barbara Ann; the people there virtually adopted her as one of their own. Immediately on arrival, the defending champion set about acclimatizing herself to the European rinks. From 6:00 am until 12 noon, each day, Barbara Ann practised. It wasn't unusual to see her petite figure with a shovel helping the sweepers remove fresh fallen snow.

Her arrival in Prague on January 7 was greeted with an outpouring of enthusiasm. One magazine reported that her photo appeared in local Prague newspapers seventeen times in three days. She was clearly as much a favourite with the Czechs as she was at home. Again Barbara Ann's performances were described as flawless. Nothing seemed to faze her. Sixty-five-kilometre-an-hour winds gusted from the river valley; an ice thaw occurred when the temperature climbed unseasonably to 5°C. Upon freezing once again, it was whipped by the wind and became bumpy and irregular. All the time her smile was glowing, seemingly transfixed on her face. When she was about to start her free-skating performance, her music unexpectedly stopped. A less-poised individual would have been shattered by all of the disruptions and less-than-ideal conditions. Not Barbara Ann! With poise much beyond her nineteen years, she simply halted her performance and waited for the problem to be solved whereupon she began once again. Cheers and applause greeted the judges' decision that Barbara Ann Scott had successfully defended her European title. This in spite of the fact that there were three competitors entered from the host country. Nonetheless, the nineteen-year-old Canadian, clad in emerald-green chiffon with shimmering sequins, and skating to "Babes in Toyland," had left an indelible memory in the minds of the twelve thousand spectators — a memory which would not be repeated since the Europeans had decided to restrict further competitions to competitors from Europe.

Meanwhile, preparations for the January 30th commencement of the Olympic games were continuing. And Barbara Ann Scott continued to be much in the public eye. The Swiss tourist offices proudly proclaimed that among the celebrities in Sankt Moritz for the games were "the Princess of Luxembourg, Barbara Ann Scott and Lord Burleigh." In Canada, the women's Athletic Federation named her the outstanding athlete of 1947 while the February 2nd edition of *Time* carried her picture on the cover.

Sankt Moritz is at an altitude of eighteen hundred metres, a fact taken into account when it was decided to use Davos, which is at the same level, as a training base. Again the weather continued to play havoc. The warm sun made for soft ice. There was a threat of the competitions being moved or cancelled. In the school figures, Barbara Ann, clad in white with red trim, a tight-fitting bonnet on her head, and wearing sun-glasses to reduce the glare of the sun on the ice, was a study in deliberation and concentration as she took the lead. The largest audience since the opening ceremonies was there to watch Barbara Ann's free-skating performance. At her tender age, she was already beginning to attain a legendary status. In spite of the uneven ice and ruts which were present from the recently concluded hockey game, Barbara Ann proceeded to thrill the huge throng with her grace and precision. When it was over, the judges only confirmed what everyone else could see for themselves. She was unmatched; she was the Olympic champion.

In Ottawa, the February 6th *Citizen* announced for all to see: "Barbara Wins It!" At the Motor Vehicles Branch, the director, Mr. Shaw, reserved the licence 48 U 1 for Barbara Ann. Actually, he had intended to set aside 48 U 1 2 but was afraid that people would simply not understand it.

But still, there was more for the Sweetheart of Canada to do. The world championships were being held in Davos within one week, the third jewel in the triple crown of figure skating on the European continent. What's more, these were considered to be even more difficult than either of the previous two since they were a test of the all-around ability of the winner. In the world's, the six compulsory figures were selected from a possibility of sixty and were not revealed until the night before, whereas the five school figures for the Olympics were well advertised for months.

With the news from the home front that she was once again selected as winner of the Lou Marsh Trophy for 1947, it was a buoyant and confident, yet intensely concentrated Barbara Ann who took to the ice at Davos. Once again she earned the title of world champion. In the space of one month, she had won the European, Olympic and world titles in some of the most trying conditions ever for such competitions.

Though she might have wished to, Barbara Ann could not return home right away. She had committed herself to a European tour. She skated before huge and adoring audiences in the capitals of Europe:

Antwerp, Oslo, Copenhagen, Paris, Berne, Lausanne and Neuchâtel. In London, prior to her departure for Canada, she brought lumps to the throats and tears to the eyes of the large turn-out at Wembley Stadium. There, she floated as if on strings to the strains of Schubert's "Ave Maria." The queen of the world met the future Queen of England when Barbara Ann joined Princess Elizabeth for tea and a viewing of her wedding gifts. Just prior to her leaving, Barbara went to Madame Tussaud's Wax Museum where she was measured for her likeness which would be placed among other "immortals." It was a tired Barbara Ann Scott who boarded the Trans-Canada Airlines North Star bound for Montreal's Dorval Airport.

With unexpected flight delays, the journey by plane took twenty-five hours. At Sydney, Nova Scotia, the plane landed at 1:00 am Tuesday, March 9. It had been expected on Monday, March 8 at 4:00 pm. In spite of the late arrival, thousands jammed the airport waiting-room area, spilling out into the parking areas, for a glimpse of their heroine. When the plane finally arrived at Montreal, at 5:00 am, the throng of reporters gathered, and matched their incessantly flashing bulbs with a cacophony of directions: "Wave this way, Barbara Ann," "Look over here, Barbara Ann," "Hold your hand up, Sweetheart," "Just one more," "This way, Barbara Ann." It was unabashed, joyful bedlam but it was still nothing to compare with the greeting awaiting Barbara Ann after her train trip to Ottawa.

The Toronto *Globe and Mail* of March 10, 1948, declared:

Spring arrived twelve days early in Ottawa on March 9, 1948. First of all, there was the sun — warm and bright. There was a breeze that was just strong enough to flutter the bunting gaily. There was an open car, covered from radiator cap to rear bumper with bright yellow daffodils. And smack in the centre, it was Barbara Ann Scott, wearing the jauntiest, sauciest, darndest little Spring hat you ever saw.

If some foreign power had decided on that afternoon, between 12:40 and 2:30 pm, to declare war on Canada, the bearer of the tidings would have had to spend quite a while in one of the parliament buildings' waiting-rooms because he wouldn't have found anyone home. "This alarming state of affairs applied in Ottawa from the Prime Minister right down the line to the third-assistant elevator operator in the Department of Agriculture," continued the *Globe*.

It was a love affair between a city and its favourite daughter. Estimates ranged as high as one hundred thousand people as crowds came out to meet her. Bands led the parade under banners proclaiming: "Barbara Ann We Love You," and "Barbara Ann, Ottawa's Sweetheart." It was a riot of sound and colour as affection permeated the spring air. "O Canada" and "Let Me Call You Sweetheart," seemed genuinely apropos. The headlines of *The Ottawa Citizen* proclaimed:

Barbara Ann Scott as a member of the Ice Capades.

54

"Today Ottawa is Yours," while offering that "no Roman conqueror returning from his greatest hour, ever got more vociferous acclaim than did the Olympic, European and world champion. But here were no victims chained to chariot wheels. Here, instead, were loyal Ottawa citizens tied to Barbara Ann's heart-strings."

Both Prime Minister Mackenzie King and Mayor Stanley Lewis greeted their champion as a proud parent would his daughter. The Prime Minister made his observation about the power of Barbara Ann's accomplishments while to the delight of the many thousands gathered below the Elgin Street platform, Mayor Lewis made Barbara Ann a Freewoman of the City. It was the first time such an honour was given to a woman and only the second ever awarded by Ottawa; the first was to Field Marshall Montgomery.

Barbara Ann Scott stayed in the news much longer; there were more parades and receptions in cities across Canada. Seldom had a citizen of any country captured the imagination of her countrymen as did this young skater. Barbara Ann Scott dolls and hats were eagerly sought by a public that somehow wanted to feel part of the life and joy given off by their princess. But nowhere was this love and affection demonstrated more than in Ottawa where it was said that:

> *Of all the long processions of Kings, Queens and Statesmen who have been greeted in the nation's capital through the years, it is doubtful if any every received the kind of welcome given to Ottawa's daughter when she returned home gracefully wearing the triple crown of World, European and Olympic champion.*
> *Today may not have been a holiday in the statutory sense — but Ottawa took a holiday just the same. It was a holiday of the heart and not of the calendar.*

55

Canadian Scene

I cannot tell the boredom from the dream
   sleep from these trees
The vacant air from the wind's pale Utopias.

but always in some hunger for the North
   a visionary yawn.
through rocks and then a gauntness going
   forth.

breathless as a child against the summer lands
   cut cold with search
a theory washing me innocent like water

and like a stretch too fragile yet for paper
I come, ungrown,
into the light that owns the immature

and makes of dispossession dread delight.
O racer winds.
   that blow, with an escape in every banner.

through Labrador such vehement loneliness
   as lies across
New Brunswick raging beyond lawyer's
   hands

cities not found and greater in the mind
woods without words
and winter on the boughs like crystal birds!

All the day I had seen the ballet on the
   hills,
the curtsey of a skier like a child's
eyelashes curving down on its cheek
but tonight when I came back I couldn't
   see anything,
for the dust lay over
and the hollows brimmed, so only when
   opened up
the wind's flare in my face like a flower
I know how fast I was going where it
   seethed and sifted,
the snowdust silted over the snow.

The importance of equipment is
commendable,
   steel-edge harness and strap
and the petal-thin cloth to strip and zip
delicate and strong, and the cap like a
   bird —
I came down through a field where my
 poles whirred

    . . .

everytime I dug them into the dark snow,
and crossed the railway and slid though
the silent town,
my skis trembled against the ice
and then I broke out of it, the speed and
silence,
and clumsily angular
I got the beer and the thaw and the fire
singing.

The importance of equipment is
commendable
I thought as I picked
the burrs of ice out of my socks and threw
my crystal mitts onto the shelf behind the
stove,

for all day I had tied such science with
delight
to feel the velvet contours flowing free
like poem or map —
to theorise and fly,
and dare a world, the mountains moving
me.

Patrick Anderson (1915 -)

Source: Dudekl, and Layton, I., Canadian
Poems (1850-1952) *(Toronto: Contact
Press, 1953).*

Cricket at the Wicket

When at the heavenly gate I bend
Saint Pete will open his little wicket,
And say: "You can't come in my friend.
You've wasted too much time at cricket,"

"Is there no cricket played up here?"
I'll anxious ask of Porter Peter;
Who will, theren't prick up his ear.
And ban me in celestial metre.

Then, Holy Peter, fare thee well
For your still gates have I no ticket;
I'll backward jog in search of   well!
Of some place where men's ghosts
Play cricket!

Source: The Toronto Mail *(15 July 1882).*

The Marathon of Hope

You did not defy
or scorn death
(that would be foolish
since no one lives forever)
but you lessoned us all
how to meet it,
making us proud and tall
in your own will.
On one metal leg, dear boy
you hopped into our hearts
and immortality.

Irving Layton

For more than two thousand years, the word *marathon* has been associated with a heroic act. During the Persian Wars, a pitched battle occurred between the Athenians and the Persians at the site of Marathon. There, the Greeks were greatly outnumbered. They were immensely aware of the pivotal struggle. Beyond Marathon, some forty kilometres distant, lay the treasured city of Athens in all of its vulnerability to the Persian hordes. The Athenian leader Miltiades summoned a messenger, Pheidippides, and instructed him to run to Sparta, two hundred and forty kilometres of rugged terrain to the south and west.

The Greek runner knew of the importance of his mission and with all of his mind and body, set out for Sparta. When the breathless and exhausted Pheidippides reached the Pelopennesian city, he was disappointed to learn that the Spartans were in the midst of religious observances. They would be unable to send assistance in time. Distraught and wanting to return to Marathon as quickly as possible with the news, he turned at once and retraced his path over the hilly and rugged terrain. At the Athenian camp, Pheidippides was met by an equally exhausted but exuberant Miltiades who informed him of the great victory the Greeks had won over the Persians at Marathon. Athens was saved, he said, "run and tell the people of our victory."

Buoyed by this turn of events, Pheidippides covered the forty kilometres from Marathon to Athens with a renewed spirit. He entered the city's gates and moved to the centre of town. At the Agora, Pheidippides earned his place in his nation's legendary history: "Rejoice, We conquer!" With those words, he collapsed and died. But he was not forgotten. Every school child throughout Greece would learn the story of their fellow

59

Terry Fox on his Marathon of Hope run.

60

citizen who put the nation's cause above his own well-being.

Twenty-five hundred years later, in a land much larger and far removed from Greece, another marathon gripped the public's imagination. A twenty-one-year-old with only one leg, the other having been lost to cancer, set out to run across that country, Canada, some five thousand kilometres, in order to demonstrate that cancer could be conquered, and to raise funds to help in that battle.

Terry Fox was a determined young man. As a youth, he had to be. Small for his age, Terry was constantly having to prove himself. In grade eight and at five foot two inches, he tried out for the Mary Hill Cobras, the school basketball team. His coach, Bob McGill, impressed with his spunk but noting his lack of size, suggested wrestling or cross-country running. Terry persisted and was the last one kept on the nine-man roster. During the summer and at almost every spare moment, Terry pestered whomever was available, but mostly his friend Doug Alward, to play basketball. In the back of his mind were the exhortations of his coach: "If you want something, you work for it because I'm not interested in mediocrity." Neither was Terry. By grade ten, regimen was paying off. He was a starting player. By grade twelve, the now-five-foot-ten-inch Terry Fox, a key guard with the Port Coquitlam Ravens, was selected co-winner of the Athlete of the Year Award. The other recipient was his close friend Doug Alward.

All things were bright and beautiful for Terry Fox. He was part of a close family; his parents, Betty and Rollie Fox, were supportive. The other children, Fred, the older by two years, and Darrel and Judith, younger by four and seven years, made it a typical family, with the occasional shouting match but always loving. When Terry was born on July 28, 1958, in Winnipeg, his father was a switch-man with the CNR. Attracted to British Columbia by the warmer climate, the family moved there in 1966, first to Surry, later to Port Coquitlam. Increasingly, as the family grew and moved from one locale to another, it seemed to draw its strength from within. There was a competitive atmosphere and sport seemed to be a natural outlet.

Terry decided to attend Simon Fraser University. Basketball beckoned and along with it an opportunity to join sport and academic study through the kinesiology program. By now Terry was gaining a reputation for giving his maximum effort whenever called upon. Through his tenacity he invariably "outgutted" his opponents. He earned a position on the Clansmen junior varsity team.

An athlete soon learns that aches and pains are associated with sport. They simply become the price one must pay. They are a commonplace occurrence. Terry thought so too and didn't really pay too much attention, for very long, to the pain in his right leg. In a game where twisting and turning, stopping and starting are integral, Terry thought that it might be a sprained ligament or perhaps a pinched cartilage. At first it was ignored but then, it became swollen and remained so for one week forcing him to use crutches. As long as he couldn't practise anyway, he decided to see an orthopaedic surgeon, Dr. Michael Piper, at the Royal Columbian Hospital. Better to have it looked at and treated now, while in the first year, than have it flare up during the next three years of his course.

Terry Fox was not prepared for what happened next. The news was harsh, upsetting, jarring, unbelievable. There was a malignant tumour . . . cancer . . . the leg would have to be amputated in four days . . . recovery would be slow . . . treatment painful . . . he might even lose his hair.

Terry Fox was shattered. All that he had held important seemed to be crumbling. His family rallied to his side, his parents wishing that there was some way to shelter their son from his affliction. Again, a former coach, Terri Flemming from Port Coquitlam High School, gave insight and direction. He brought a copy of *Runner's World* magazine, one which featured a story about Dick Traum, an amputee who had competed in the New York marathon. It was the night before the operation and already the wheels were beginning to turn.

That was March 9, 1977. The leg was amputated above the knee. Three weeks later, he was outfitted with an artificial leg. In three more weeks, the determined young man had mastered the golf swing and began thinking of joining a wheelchair basketball team. Within one month he was able to play twenty-seven holes of golf on a recreation-size course. The physical accomplishments were important to Terry but he was far from pleased. His regular visit to the clinic for chemotherapy brought him into contact with people of all ages and sizes, all with the pain of cancer in common. He was maturing beyond his years. He was to joke later that the one good thing about the chemotherapy was that after his straight hair fell out, it grew back in curly.

As he adjusted to his new life, the image of the amputee marathoner returned. The wheelchair basketball was fun but it wasn't the same. He had to be moving. He would try running; he would prepare himself the only way he knew how. Once again, Terry thought of Bob McGill. He was now a vice-principal at Hastings Junior High School, where there was a running track. Ironically, Bob McGill was himself a victim of skin cancer at this time. He listened attentively to Terry's plans and offered encouragement and support. And so in February of 1979, under the cover of darkness, Terry began his training. His first attempt at running was a modest half-kilometre. But then, he practically had to reinvent running — two shuffles with his good leg and a plant with the wooden one. At the same time, Terry began to read the *Bible*, hoping to gain some insight into his plight, and strength for his plans.

For eighteen months, Terry was possessed by his idea. His training was a reflection of the strong will which he had developed. It was painful. At times, his stump was raw and bloody. Toe-nails became black and blue and

62

fell off. For more than one hundred days, he continued his training with an intense zeal. Now his plans were taking shape and on October 15, 1979, he wrote the following letter to the Canadian Cancer Society:

Dear Sir:

My name is Terry Fox. I am twenty-one years old, and I am an amputee. I lost my right leg two and a half years ago due to cancer.

The night before my amputation, my former basketball coach brought me a magazine with an article on an amputee who ran in the New York Marathon. It was then when I decided to meet this challenge head on and not only overcome my disability, but conquer it in such a way that I could never look back and say it disabled me.

But I soon realized that would only be half my quest, for as I went through the sixteen months of the physically and emotionally draining ordeal of chemotherapy, I was rudely awakened by the feelings that surrounded and coursed throughout the cancer clinic. There were the faces with the brave smiles, and the ones who had given up smiling. There were the feelings of hopeful denial, and the feelings of despair. My quest would not be a selfish one. I could not leave knowing these faces and feelings would still exist, even though I would be set free from mine. Somewhere the hurting must stop . . . and I was determined to take myself to the limit for this cause.

I feel now is the time to make good my promise. I have been training for eight months, running on an artificial leg. Starting with a half a mile, I have now worked up to thirteen and a half miles a day, adding a half mile weekly.

From the beginning the going was extremely difficult, and I was facing chronic ailments foreign to runners with two legs, in addition to the common physical strains felt by all dedicated athletes. But these problems are now behind me, as I have either out-persisted or learnt to deal with them. I feel strong not only physically, but more important, emotionally. Soon I will be adding one full mile each week, and coupled with the weight training I have been doing three times a week, by April next year I will be ready to achieve something that for me was once only a distant dream reserved for the world of miracles: to run across Canada to raise money for the fight against cancer.

The running I can do, even if I have to crawl every last mile. But there are some barriers I cannot overcome alone. I need your help, your sponsorship, to provide the means to sustain myself and one other who has consented to put aside those five months to be my companion. We will need transportation to Newfoundland, a camper-type vehicle to meet us there, and money for food, gas and other necessities. My three years in university have quite aptly drained me financially, and just the thought that I will require twenty-six pairs of running shoes for myself and my running companion makes my now dwindling account crawl deeper into its hole.

Please consider my idea carefully, and notify me if you come to any decisions, good or bad. My number is listed below and a message can be left at my home any time of the day.

We need your help. The people in cancer clinics all over the world need people who believe in miracles. I'm not a dreamer, and I'm not saying that this will initiate any kind of definite answer or cure to cancer, but I believe in miracles.

I have to.

Yours sincerely, Terry Fox.

When an impressed but somewhat sceptical Blair Mackenzie from the British Columbia and Yukon division of the Canadian Cancer Society was asked for sponsorship, he suggested that if Terry could lay the foundation for his run, the society would do what it could. That small bit of encouragement was all that Terry needed. With the help of his family, he organized a dance and raised some twenty-five hundred dollars for travelling expenses. He embarked on a massive training program while canvassing industry, all the while determined to carry on the battle for the people left behind in the cancer ward. By the end of the first week in April, 1980, Terry had run 5,083 km training for his run across Canada. Ford Motor Company provided a van; Imperial Oil Limited donated gas while Adidas gave shoes.

On April 12, viewers across Canada who watched *The National* newscast were able to get their first view of Terry. He was in St. John's, Newfoundland, ready to begin his run across the country. There he was dipping his leg into the Atlantic in the harbour and filling a jug with water. His goal was to dip his leg again into the Pacific and pour the water there, too. It was a symbolic gesture but one which the tenacious Terry aimed to keep. At kilometre 0 of the Trans-Canada Highway Mayor Dorothy Wyatt gave him an official send-off. Terry Fox had started on his Marathon of Hope.

It wasn't the best of times to be running in Newfoundland. During the first four days, high winds, gale force at times, rain, wind and wet snow buffeted Terry. Ignoring all, he hopped along followed by Doug Alward in the van. One hundred and fifty kilometres to Come By Chance were covered in four days. More misfortune plagued him, however. His artificial leg, unable to hold up to the strain, broke at the knee-joint. It simply was not made for such heavy-duty pounding. Undaunted, Terry put on a substitute leg which he had packed and continued on his crusade. The damaged leg was sent to Fredericton to be repaired, free of charge, by the War Amps organization.

As news of the young one-legged athlete travelled about this island province, Newfoundlanders opened their hearts and wallets to his cause. Refreshments, words of encouragement ("you sure got the guts Terry"), and up to seven thousand dollars per day raised for cancer helped him to keep going along his arduous journey. It was far from easy. Not even Olympic marathoners would attempt to run forty-two kilometres per day — and that was with two good legs. As well, he had to contend with pain previously unknown. Cysts had developed on the stump from the constant friction. The mental and physical exhaustion caused him to have jags of crying but, strangely enough, it

Terry Fox along a lonely stretch of highway.

seemed as if the agitated and emotional state kept him going. In twenty-five days he had covered 927 kilometres in Newfoundland. On May 6, he boarded the ferry for North Sydney, Nova Scotia. The Cancer Society was some twenty-five thousand dollars richer. Terry's crusade was catching on; the Four Seasons Hotel challenged 999 other corporations to sponsor the run at two dollars each mile. Now it was being spoken of as the Ten Million Dollar Run!

Throughout Nova Scotia, Terry Fox felt pain but refused to see any doctors. As far as he was concerned, none was an amputee who had ever tried to run across Canada and so no good advice could be offered — only sympathy and suggestions to stop running and Terry wasn't having any of that. In other respects, too, the Nova Scotia portion of the run was somewhat disappointing. Someone who was a little less tenacious might have dropped out. While a CBC crew drove alongside Terry, a tractor-trailer smashed into it. Upset by the near tragedy, Terry could run no more that day, but did find time to visit the injured CBC workers in the hospital.

But his morale was beginning to sag. The run was attracting little of the attention that Terry had hoped for when he began. And the little attention in the media meant fewer donations to the cancer fund. Where he had hoped to raise some fifty thousand dollars in Nova Scotia, only eight thousand dollars would be realized. More publicity was needed and so the decision was made to detour south some 280 kilometres to Halifax

where the media exposure would help to publicize his run. It would also mean that he could swing into Dartmouth where his parents would be waiting to see him for the first time since he left British Columbia. It was the tonic Terry needed. The reunion lasted until Terry reached Springhill, forty-one days and 1,563 kilometres into his run.

Now Terry's spirits were uplifted. They continued to soar on the ferry ride to Prince Edward Island where the captain collected three hundred and fifty dollars from his passengers and crew. There was more. The Islanders opened up their hearts to the young man they had heard so much about. The Maritime publicity was beginning to reap its rewards. Even though it was 5:00 am, a P.E.I. radio station was there to meet him as the ferry docked and followed him to Charlottetown, broadcasting every step. It appeared that no one could be home on the island since the route was lined with what seemed to be the whole population, all straining to get a glimpse of Terry and wish him well. It was a beautiful sight for a now-buoyant Terry.

On June 4, it was into New Brunswick. Terry, feeling stronger as the run continued, was now averaging forty-eight kilometres per day. Now he was joined by his brother Darrel who decided to pass up his graduation in order to join Terry. The people of the province provided Terry with an unforgettable home-town-style welcome. At one location, Petitcodiac residents paid ten dollars a plate, donated their own food and raised more than one thousand dollars at a community supper.

A determined Terry Fox, his support van following him.

In some ways, Terry Fox's run was much like the geography of the land he was crossing, filled with peaks and valleys. The sheer physical demands this young man was making on his body day after day caused a numbness and aching that at times couldn't be endured. A less-committed person would have given up his idea long ago. Now it was June and raining as he entered Quebec. Clad in a raincoat, he was constantly being forced off the road by unaware motorists. His efforts had been ignored by the media and the provincial police were seemingly ignorant of the run. They gently suggested that it would be safer to run on a secondary road. Through the disappointment, Terry was able to cover 160 kilometres in four days, but to raise only thirty-five dollars. Montreal provided a brief respite. He was escorted there by Alouette football player Don Sweet, and met by Mayor Drapeau. Terry managed to spend a restless two days with relatives, pleased to see them but at the same time, anxious to continue while the weather was good.

On June 29 he entered Ontario, crossing the Perly Bridge at Hawkesbury. What a refreshing change! It was as if a signal had been given that the virtual anonymity of the run had been banished, never to surface again. Balloons were released, a band blared, people cheered and the Ontario Provincial Police provided a personal escort throughout the province, his entrance to the next city or town being announced by excited police sirens. It was hot, above 30°C, causing Terry to cherish 4:00 am when the mornings were cool, quiet, windless and refreshing — a perfect time to run.

Along the Ontario portion of the Trans-Canada Highway, he shuffled and thumped his way with his unique gait, occasionally taking time out to give himself a drink and a lube job to ease the rubbing of the artificial leg as well as the belt around his waist which gave the leg some support. Along any quiet stretch, his tape recorder wailed out the plaintive singing of Hank Williams' "Jambalaya" and "Your Cheatin' Heart." The timing of the run couldn't have been better. July 1 was Canada's birthday. People were in a patriotic mood and Terry Fox was appealing more and more as a national symbol of hope, a folk hero. In Ottawa, he was enthusiastically greeted in the Sparks Street Mall, received a standing ovation in Landsdowne Park where he performed the ceremonial kick-off at a Rough Rider game, pivoting with his artificial limb and kicking the ball with his good one. His visit was capped by a meeting with Prime Minister Trudeau who himself was only beginning to be caught up in the love and admiration a nation was beginning to feel for her son.

By now, approximately 3,200 kilometres had been painfully passed by the young man who was now part of the consciousness of all Canadians. Highway buses passed him only to be waiting up ahead with a collection from among the passengers. Cheques and cash were continually being thrust into the hands of the youth by motorists having seen him along the way. There was one, of many, who

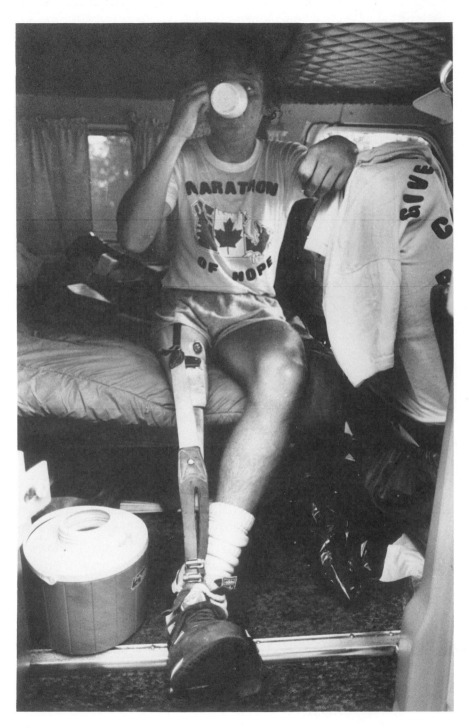

Terry Fox in a moment of rest.

on her way to church said she would offer prayers for him, all the while hardly able to speak because of the tears in her eyes. But there was pain too; always there was pain. After so much running, some five centimetres of muscle was added to his stump. A new leg was constructed in Ottawa and shipped to Terry.

The young, curly-haired youth was like a driven man. The fatigue and pain alone would have been enough to dissuade a lesser individual who had no cause, but Terry kept on. On July 10, he was in Oshawa, drained. Rising early, he ran just three kilometres. He was exhausted. He would try to do one more, again pushing himself beyond his limits. As if by magic, his parents appeared among the crowd, waiting for their son at a street corner. They had been flown in from Vancouver by *The Toronto Star* for the surprise reunion. It couldn't have come at a better time for the exhausted crusader.

The reception in Toronto could only be described as tumultuous, "the kind of welcome we give the Queen," one said. Crowds ten and twelve deep lined the streets to see him. Lumps in throats were common as the young man with this shuffle, shuffle, thump movement and the painfully determined look on his face came into view. Prior to his entrance into Nathan Phillips Square, in front of Toronto's City Hall, he was joined by the Toronto Maple Leafs' Captain, Darryl Sittler. Terry had made two requests of the Ontario Cancer Society people upon entering that province: he would like to meet Sittler, and he would like to meet Bobby Orr. The Leaf had surprised Terry by showing up at his hotel room after breakfast wearing shorts, running shoes and a Terry Fox T-shirt asking, "Anyone want to go for a run?" There were ten thousand people standing in the square seeking a glimpse of Terry and ready to offer him their support. Now Terry was on a high. Not only had Sittler joined him for that phase of the run but so too had his brothers, Fred and Darrel, and his constant companion Doug Alward.

If ever an individual captured the heart of a city, this was him. This superstar, this hero of Canada threw out the first pitch at the Blue Jay-Cleveland baseball game, visited and dined at the CN Tower, flew to Niagara Falls. All the while, he was able to use the Four Seasons Hotel, accommodations provided by that chain, as his central Toronto base. It was as if people were trying in small ways to repay the young man for his unselfish display of goodness and sacrifice for others. On July 13, Terry continued along the Lakeshore Road to south-western Ontario. Above him, atop the CN Tower, was an illuminated sign saying simply, "Terry Fox."

Now it was time to try to re-establish his routine of forty-two kilometres per day, rising at 4:00 am, running until 8:00 am followed by breakfast, a two-hour rest and more running. Two weeks later, Terry returned to Toronto in order to swing north. Now his second wish came true; he met Bobby Orr. It was soon obvious that each had an immense amount of admiration for the other. Since Terry had to run through Parry Sound, Orr's home-town, the former hockey star suggested that he drop in on Orr's parents. To Fox's huge delight and surprise, Orr had made arrangements to present Terry with the sweater he wore during the 1976 Canada Cup hockey series. It was a matching gift for Terry; he had previously been given Darryl Sittler's number 27 Maple Leaf sweater.

July 28 was Terry's twenty-second birthday but it was spent pretty well like any other day, on the road running along number 11 highway, north of Barrie. There was simply no time for parties for this intense young man with a mission. He was afraid that he wouldn't make it to Vancouver before the

Terry Fox along a busy highway.

snows fell. Admiration and the adulation continued to precede him and follow in his wake. Inmates at the Beaver Dam Penitentiary, in awe of his courage, raised nine hundred dollars. General Motors and a group of British Columbia-based business-men, the Jim Pattison Group, donated a luxurious seven-metre mobile home to be used as his home base. It came in handy as Terry headed into Northern Ontario where the cooler weather was fast approaching. People seemed to be only too anxious to help; when a small spring broke in his artificial leg at Sault Ste. Marie, radio appeals brought out a welder to fix it immediately.

At Terrace Bay, he found time to renew acquaintances with a ten-year-old boy from Welland, Ontario, Greg Scott. Like Terry, he too was an amputee who had lost his leg to cancer. His chemotherapy treatments had left him bald — and self-conscious to the point where he constantly wore his hat. Terry always seemed to be able to find someone worse off than himself, someone he might be able to help directly or indirectly. The two chatted with each other, Terry continually trying to draw the youngster out of himself. Each removed his artificial limb and prepared to go for a swim. Young Greg completely forgot himself, enjoying everything immensely. He splashed Terry, something which brought howls of protest. All of this was a huge sacrifice for Terry who was not a good swimmer and would only go into the water for something special. But the rest was good for Terry too. Not only was he

able to see Greg again and be reassured that the youngster was fine, the diversion also allowed him time to recover from the frequent inflammations he was experiencing.

It was August 29 when Terry became aware of an even greater discomfort in his chest. But he was used to living with pain during his Marathon of Hope. He shrugged it off. Feeling somewhat more comfortable on the 30th, he covered thirty-seven kilometres followed by thirty-four on the 31st. But he laboured strenuously, racked by pain during his last kilometre, the 5,343 kilometre of his journey. The man who had ignored doctors, now called for one.

The news was bleak, stark, devastating . . . the cancer had returned, this time to the lungs. On September 8, 1980, the run was over. On June 28, 1981, one month before his twenty-third birthday, Terry Fox died.

The ten-month period between the cessation of the run and Terry Fox's death was, perhaps, the greatest demonstration of this nation's love and attachment for one of its citizens. He died in a year dedicated to the handicapped — and yet everyone thought of the one-legged runner as anything but. Within days of the announcement of the return of the cancer, hundreds offered to finish the Marathon of Hope but Terry and his family steadfastly refused to consider such a request. The 5000 kilometres plus would stand as a testimony to Terry . . . as would the money raised. Terry had originally hoped for an average of one dollar per Canadian citizen to be raised and used exclusively for research into the dreaded disease. It was time now to give him some assistance. The CTV network, within weeks of Terry's relapse, conducted a telethon, raising more than ten and one-half million dollars in pledges. People from all across Canada began to send in their contributions to cancer units in every city. At his death, well over twenty-four million dollars had been raised.

Honours and messages poured into the home of the youngster whose courage had touched

Sports Hall of Famer Red Foster with the parents of Terry Fox at the unveiling of a painting of Terry.

people from every walk of life. The Prime Minister, the Queen, World War Two-ace Douglas Bader, himself an amputee, sent messages. Others came from as far away as Israel, Saudi Arabia, Nepal, Malaysia and the United States. The Canadian Governor General, Edward Schreyer, flew to Port Coquitlam to invest Terry with the Order of Canada; the British Columbia Premier, William Bennett, conferred the Order of the Dogwood, the highest honour his province could bestow.

Still the recognition continued. *The Toronto Star* awarded him the prestigious Lou Marsh Trophy, given annually to the Canadian Athlete of the Year. The Government of Canada, after intense public pressure to bend its rules announced plans to offer a postage stamp in his memory, even though it was against policy to issue stamps while the person honoured was still alive. In addition, it was announced throughout Canada on September 13, 1981, that ten-kilometre runs would be held to allow people to sponsor entrants and raise money for cancer research. Terry was inducted into Canada's Sports Hall of Fame; the British Columbia and Ontario governments each contributed one million dollars for cancer research. The Canadian Press named Terry as the Man of the Year for 1980. In the United States, where his run was followed closely, telegrams of support came from many, including Senator Edward Kennedy. The American Cancer Society presented Terry with its highest honour, the Sword Award. Again, the Federal Government of Canada announced yet another tribute to the young runner. In his name, two hundred and fifty scholarships would be offered, the money to be raised from the interest on a five million dollar trust fund. Plans were also announced for a national youth centre in Terry Fox's name in Ottawa. On the outskirts of Ottawa, in Orleans, a school was dedicated in his name while a mountain in British Columbia and the last eighty-kilometre stretch of the highway run by Terry would perpetuate the memory of his selfless feat. The road from Nipigon to Thunder Bay was aptly named The Terry Fox Courage Highway. On April 12, 1990, ten years after he began his run, Betty and Rolly Fox were joined by their other children Fred, Judith and Darrell, and Doug Alward, to unveil a commemorative plaque at the spot where Terry had dipped his artificial leg in the cold, Atlantic waters of St. John's harbour.

When he died on June 28, 1981, there was the feeling of a national loss throughout the land. It's doubtful that any person in Canadian history had ever been more a part of the nation's psyche. It was as if more than a good friend, more like a spiritual essence of nationhood, was being withdrawn, that someone very close to all was missing. Almost universally there seemed to be the conviction that somehow a way had to be found to remind the future of the time when one individual decided to do something rather than sit around looking for sympathy. Government flags throughout the country flew at half-mast, an honour usually reserved for statesmen and politicians of national

The artist viewing her work.

rank. The fly-past of the Canadian Armed Forces Voodoos at the funeral was in the traditional missing-man formation. Prime Minister Trudeau aptly summed up the public's feelings when he described Terry Fox as, "a young man whose courage and awesome determination inspired this nation as no one else has done." But perhaps everyone's feelings for the young man, who was now a legend in his own time, were best illustrated by a poem from St. Theresa's grade-six class in Toronto:

Oh Terry you must be the guy
Who invented the word "try"
And as for the phrase "never quit"
I'm sure that you discovered it.

In Memoriam

Oblit. Christmas, MDCCCLXXXIII

Reaper, could'st thou not pass by?
Thou passest none. Oh! cruel death,
We come and go like fleeting breath.
We little dream when thou art nigh.

In vain the Christmas Day was bright,
The winds went sobbing as they passed
That Christmas morn: alas, the last
Soon faded into sorrow's night.

From day to day we miss thy face,
And look to meet thee in our halls,
But memory soon the truth recalls,
And points us to they empty place.

And when the game is going fast,
Against the college on the green,
We'll miss thee most, For thou has been,
Our fleetest foot, Sure to the last.

And now, farewell, we sadly mourn
For thou art gone, ah! all too soon.
The day has ended at the noon,
And from us thou art rudely torn.

'Varsity
Edgar Norman Hughes

Source: The Toronto Mail *(2 February 1883), p.9.*

The Decision

*(To L.R., a college athlete who died
May, 1923)*

*You left the field and no one heard
A murmur from you. We,
With burning look and stubborn word,
Challenged the Referee —*

*Why he forbade you to complete
The run, hailing you back
Before your firm and eager feet
Were half-way round the track;*

*Unless he had contrived, instead,
To start you on a race,
With an immortal course ahead,
And daybreak on your face.*

E.J. Pratt

Source: Frye, Northrop, editor, The
Collected Poems of E.J. Pratt, *2nd edition
(Toronto: MacMillan Co. of Canada, 1962).*

The Greatest

One doesn't naturally think of basketball as a Canadian game. Yet the fact remains that James Naismith, its inventor, was from the Ottawa Valley town of Almonte, and a student at Springfield College, when he introduced it to the world. The year was 1891. Naismith's new game caught on quickly, perhaps nowhere more so than in Canada where it spread throughout the land wherever a YMCA happened to be.

One doesn't think, also, that the greatest team ever to play the game was Canadian. That is, unless one knows of the world-famous Edmonton Grads. For twenty-five years, from 1915-1940, this group of women were acknowledged world champions — the focus of Edmonton life. They were the darlings of the Canadian public, as much in demand in Toronto as they were in Chicago or Paris. Their leader was a much loved and respected individual, John "Percy" Page, a teacher who became a member of the Alberta legislature and later lieutenant-governor of that province. The Percy Page Centre for Sport, Alberta's administrative centre for sport, is located in St. Albert and named in his honour. When the Edmonton Grads decided to disband in 1940, the team, using a variety of different players throughout its history, had played 548 games and won 524. They were undefeated in Canadian championship play, had competed at four Olympics — had thirty-one contests there and won them all — played twenty-four games in various European tours and were undefeated. Of one hundred and twenty games for North American title play, they won one hundred and fourteen. Simply and succinctly put, they were the greatest!

One couldn't help to reminisce about the Grads when they were ready to play their last series for the Underwood Trophy and the North American championship in 1940. The fans who had thrilled to their play for the last twenty-five years were now reunited with their favourites. Memories flowed!

"Go west young man" was an oft-repeated bit of advice during the late-nineteenth and early-twentieth century. It was a land full of promise and hope where one could, through initiative and hard work, fulfil dreams and ambitions. When John Page arrived in Edmonton to be principal at McDougall High School, he was full of hope and dreams.

79

Already, he had graduated from Queen's University in Kingston and found teaching positions in New Brunswick and St. Thomas, Ontario. Then the West with its opportunities beckoned. Page moved to Edmonton with his young bride.

It was 1914. War clouds loomed on the horizon. Soon, the Great War would begin. Most schools in Canada at that time taught Physical Training, or PT as it was more popularly known. Ever since 1910 it had consisted of much marching, drill and rifle shooting. Almost everything else was neglected. The schools were the one agency where all people would, at one time or another in their lives, have a common exposure, and thus the drill during these times made good sense from a national security point of view.

For Page, however, there was another way. During his days in New Brunswick, not far from Springfield, the new game of basketball had impressed him. It had so many benefits, but best of all it seemed to be enjoyed immensely both by the participants and the spectators. Page decided to introduce it to the high school as a compulsory part of the Physical Training classes. He also decided to have representative boys' and girls' teams. The story made the rounds that Page flipped a coin, but in any event, his assistant, a young bachelor, chose to coach the boys' team. Page was left with the girls. It was jokingly stated that since he had been married for three years, he understood women and thus the decision was much easier.

With no gym in the school, the girls were forced to play outdoors. It was a somewhat different game in the early years. Whatever floor was available was divided into three zones. Each team placed two players in one zone wherein they could take a maximum of three bounces with the ball before passing it off. The two players in the opponents' net area were the only ones who could score. After each basket there was a jump ball or a tip off at centre court. Thus a smaller, faster team might have the advantage while working the ball up the floor towards the opponents' goal, but that could be offset by the taller team having the advantage at centre court. The Commercial High School team learned its lessons well during the 1914 season, winning the city championship. The decision was made to enter the provincial play-downs the next year. As a matter of fact, the girls decided that they enjoyed the experience so much that they wanted to play together after graduation. Page formed the Gradettes to go along with his own team, later known as the Grads. With enthusiasm and skill, the young ladies from Edmonton swept every team in the province to win every provincial title from 1915 to 1920. To the surprise of many, they had lost it in 1921 to the University of Alberta. Page's reaction was that perhaps his girls needed new horizons to challenge them.

The Grads were scarcely known outside Alberta but 1922 was to remove their national anonymity. East-west competition was becoming a reality, aided by the railroads and encouraged by a public that wanted to know how their favourites compared with teams across the land. The Eskimos had gone east in 1921 to do battle with the Argonauts in the Grey Cup game, the first time a western team had ever challenged for the trophy. In 1922, plans were made for the Grads to travel to London, Ontario, to play that city's Shamrocks for the Dominion championship.

But first, there were problems to iron out. Each team played according to different rules: London used men's rules — five players per team, movement allowed anywhere by anyone and shooting by all. The Grads had never played such a game. They had only six players. With such a limited substitution capability they would be at a definite disadvantage. It was therefore decided that the fairest way to resolve the dilemma would be to play two games, one under each set of rules with total points to decide the championship. That settled, the Grads now had to raise the necessary funds to make the 8,000-kilometre trip. London could guarantee six hundred dollars. Each player could contribute twenty-five dollars plus their own packed lunches. The rest was made up from sundry contributions from Edmonton citizens as well as Page's pocket. Two thousand dollars were raised; the western champions would be the first basketball team from the west to travel east to London to play for a Canadian title.

The Grads, by this time all graduates of McDougall High, were a sight to behold when they took to the court. In their colours of black and gold, they wore loose middies and knee-length bloomers, hair-bands to keep their eyes free, heavy woollen stockings, pads covering the knees. Nellie Perry, a stenographer, was the team's leading shooter. The other forward spot was played by Daisy Johnson, a teacher at Irma High School. At centre was Eleanor Mountifield, a bookkeeper, while Daisy's younger sister, Dorothy Johnson, played at side centre. At the guard position were Connie Smith and Winnie Martin, who as well as being the oldest player and captain, was reputed to be the fastest typist in Canada, a title actually earned in competition.

The Edmonton team demonstrated that they knew the game of basketball. In the first game under the western rules, the Grads shocked the one thousand followers at the London Armouries. The spectators who had come hoping to see a Shamrock victory were in a state of subdued but respectful awe. The Grads outscored the eastern team by a 41-8 score. The thirty-three-point lead would stand them in good stead since the second game would be under eastern rules, something that the Grads had never played before. In the second game at the Armouries, this time before fifteen hundred spectators, the Shamrocks attained a measure of revenge, winning the game 21-8. It wasn't enough to win the title but enough that their followers could blame the first game loss on the unfamiliar girls' rules.

Whatever anyone thought, one thing was certain: Edmonton had won the series and could claim the title of Dominion Champions. Upon their return to a jammed CNR station in Edmonton, the Grads were given a boisterous welcome. They were Edmonton's first Canadian champions and the city was proud. The parade up Jasper Avenue gave their fellow citizens a chance to see and pay tribute to the "best in Canada." Grateful for this welcome honour, the city gave medals to each player, which they proudly wore at the breakfast with the mayor at the Macdonald Hotel.

With the beginning of the 1923 season, it was obvious that the Grads must learn to play the faster, eastern or boys' game. They practised diligently and once again made it to the Dominion finals. Again, London provided the competition. This time, however, the game was in Edmonton. There, before their home-town fans, the Grads again proved their superiority; they were simply the best in Canada — and by quite a margin. Once again, new challenges were needed. This time, the vehicle would be the new Underwood Trophy.

When the Grads had wanted to travel to London in 1922, they were short of money. Captain Winnie Martin had an idea. She had entered and won a typewriting contest and, as the fastest typist in Canada, she used an Underwood product at work. She contacted the Underwood president, J. J. Seitz, with a request for financial assistance. She also offered to change the Grads name to the Underwood Flyers in return. Mr. Seitz declined to involve his company directly but did donate some $250 of his own personal money. In addition, he was so taken with the enthusiasm of the team that he travelled to London to watch the team perform. When

Cleveland came to Edmonton to inaugurate an international championship for which there was no award, Seitz donated the Underwood Trophy, a symbol of the North American championship under men's rules. He set up a board of trustees: Alexandrine Gibb of Toronto, Adrian Brennan of Hartford, Harry Wilson of Chicago and Percy Page of Edmonton. For the inaugural series, Edmonton, as Canadian title-holder, was selected as one team; the other was from Cleveland. Edmonton was proposed as the site of the match, but Cleveland insisted that it could only make the long trek north if eighteen hundred dollars were guaranteed to cover expenses. That was an awful lot of money and Edmonton's prospects of becoming the first North American champion seemed gloomy. It was Deacon Whyte who saved the day. Whyte, a sports promoter and coach of the Edmonton Eskimos football team, had seen the girls play and was greatly impressed. He offered to put up the guarantee. In addition, the incredulous Grads were told that the team could keep two-thirds of any profit generated.

Revitalized now, Page instructed his charges to practise twice a week: one and one-half hours each practice followed by a mile run and practice games with men's teams. It was an unheard-of regimen for young women in sport; there were always constant fears about the possible loss of femininity and of becoming muscle-bound molls due to such strenuous activity.

Nonetheless, when the evening of June 12, 1923, arrived, almost five thousand

Edmontonians filled the arena to watch the contest. Thousands more were beside their crystal sets listening to a play-by-play on CJCA. When the Grads won the first game of the series 34-20, all were ecstatic. Two nights later, they were again victors by a 19-13 score. Page's Princesses were the queens of North America. Not only that. Because of the huge public following, they had justified Deacon Whyte's faith in them. Their share of the gate was an amazing twenty-four hundred dollars! At three more defences of the new trophy that year, the successful Grads raised eleven thousand dollars — enough to afford a trip to the 1924 Olympic Games in Paris, France. Basketball was not an official sport at the Games, but the Grads, in a superb demonstration, won each of six contests played against European competition. They could easily make the claim to be world champions.

First Canadian Champions — the Grads of 1922. Back: Daisy Johnson, Nellie Perry, Eleanor Mountifield (Capt.), Dorothy Johnson and Connie Smith. Front: J. Percy Page and Winnie Martin.

By 1925, Hattie Hopkins, Elsie Bennis and Kate MacRae had joined Mary Dunn, Daisy and Dorothy Johnson, and Connie Smith. Each team seemed to be measured against the standard of the previous one, a comparison likely only to develop into an argument. The Grads continued to practise with boys' teams in an attempt to stretch their limits. Indeed they had to be ready to play under a variety of circumstances. When they travelled to Winnipeg in February of 1925, the game was played on a stage in a theatre. They were much in demand now with invitations from Vancouver, Victoria, New Westminster and Kamloops in British Columbia. They easily won all contests.

Paris Olympic Team — the Grads of 1924. Back: Eleanor Mountifield, Connie Smith, J. Percy Page, Abbie Scott and Daisy Johnson. Front: Nellie Perry, Mary Dunn, Winnie Martin (Capt.) and Dorothy Johnson.

When they were challenged for the Canadian championship by the YMHA women's team of Toronto, the eastern feeling was that if any team could defeat the Grads, it was this one. The YMHA girls had won all but one game that year and that loss was only by one basket. In addition, they had the outstanding all-around athlete, Bobbie "Fanny" Rosenfeld. Regardless, the Grads won the two-game, total-point series 35-11, their fourth consecutive Canadian championship.

With the Canadian portion of their schedule finished, the Grads now turned their attention to American teams and the defence of the Underwood Trophy. The Chicago Lakeviews were disposed of by a 52-27 score; the Minnesota Ascensions were defeated in an 84-12 romp (they did not even provide a light work-out for Percy Page's world-champion Grads). Both victories were at home but when the Grads were invited south to defend their title, they gladly accepted. One such time was when they travelled to Oklahoma, to play a team from Guthrie. A huge send-off was given at the train station in Edmonton. Upon arrival in Guthrie, an equally boisterous reception and celebration were given to the Queens of the North. The results were the same: the Grads won the two-game series by a combined score of 45-19. At Fort Worth, Texas, an all-star aggregation was defeated 47-6, while in Pasadena, California, the Grads won a 27-7 decision. Wherever the Grads went, there was amazement that the game of basketball could be so well played. Most cities felt that they had pretty good local talent but up against the Underwood champions, there was no comparison . . . . When the Edmonton team defeated one from San Francisco by a 62-2 score, newspapers "had nothing but praise for the plucky Edmonton team." It was a four-week tour, an immense success, and not incidentally, a successful defence of the Underwood trophy, wherever the game was played.

In 1926, the Grads continued their dominance. Now they were outfitted in new black and gold jerseys, shorts and sox . . . a Chicago paper wrote that Connie Smith was in the same category relative to her sport that Babe Ruth was to baseball or Red Grange to football. High tribute indeed! In search of new fields to conquer, the Grads made their way east. Games in Winnipeg, Chicago and Connecticut were won easily. On to Cleveland, Ohio. There the Grads were to play the Newman-Sterns for the Underwood Trophy. As always, it was stipulated that, should the champions lose, they would be given an opportunity to regain the title.

Up to this point the Grads and their followers had become very matter of fact about their winning ways. After all, they had gone through fifty-three consecutive Underwood Trophy wins. No one expected that they might even come close to losing. No one except Cleveland that is. They had been practising with increasing intensity and purpose in preparation for meeting the Grads. The games, billed as classic confrontations, drew ten thousand spectators eagerly looking for the upset. It came. The first game was won by Cleveland 23-16. They exhibited a very controlled game that prevented the Grads from dictating the style of play. The Grads, strong team that they were, bounced back to win the second by a 26-21 score. The Cleveland team was clearly trying to establish their type of game; they held the Grads to ten points in the third contest while scoring fifteen themselves. Now the ten thousand Cleveland supporters eagerly looked forward to what they hoped would be the deciding match, the one which would give them the Underwood Trophy and the title of North American Champions. The basketball was superlative, albeit low scoring. Cleveland won the fourth game 13-8, the series 72-60. The Queens of Basketball had been dethroned. For the first time since 1923, the trophy rested in a city other than Edmonton. A tired and disappointed collection of basketballers made their way to the train station where they left for Toronto to defend their Canadian championship. They were already talking rematch.

The Grads were still in a state of shock when they took the court against the Toronto Lakesides. They suffered their third consecutive loss! They were five points down, 24-19, in their two-game, total-points series. It appeared as if their world had come apart. Something had to be done in order to regain their winning form. Page had scheduled a game with London the following evening. He decided that he would play his substitutes more, not only to give them an opportunity to play but also to perk up the older players.

It worked. Against London, the Grads once again seemed to hit their stride with a 40-15 victory. It seemed to be just what was needed. Their second game with Toronto was won 27-6, the round 56-30.

Now they had a new winning streak. The fatigue seemed to have left them and, on their arrival in Edmonton, they immediately took up their option and challenged Cleveland to another match for the Underwood Trophy. What should have been a straightforward transaction, was not. The Cleveland team procrastinated for a long time and eventually refused to honour the agreement. It was too inconvenient, they said, for another match to take place so soon. The girls all had job commitments and couldn't practise to the pitch necessary for a championship series whenever they were challenged. Eventually the president of Underwood was asked to intercede. It was felt that the trustees were too involved with the games and a completely impartial arbiter was needed. J. J. Seitz ruled that, since Cleveland refused to play the Grads for the title, the trophy would revert to the Edmonton team. Immediately a match was arranged with the St. Louis Clothiers, a very tall team with a record of one hundred and thirty-seven wins and only two defeats. The out-sized Grads played with new-found life, hoping that they were deserving champions although prefering to win their titles on the court. The Grads won both games and the round 43-22. In their minds, however, they would not be satisfied until they were able to play the Cleveland team once again.

But the Grads were too busy to spend much time worrying about things over which they had no control. Another successful season in 1927 and 1928 culminated with the Grads' visit to the Amsterdam Olympics. Basketball was still not part of the official Games program but, in conjunction with the Olympics, a series of contests with Europeans was arranged.

Residents and visitors to Amsterdam would have many memories of Canada after the Olympics of 1928. Some would remember the world's fastest human, winner of two gold medals, Percy Williams. For others it was the Matchless Six, Canada's winning first women's track-and-field team. Still others recalled the sculpture by the Canadian R. Tait McKenzie entitled *Joy of Effort* embedded in the wall of the Olympic stadium. To many, however, it was the remarkable play of another group of Canadians, the Edmonton Grads. They seemed to be able to perform the impossible with a basketball.

The Grads were due to leave Montreal aboard the *Regina* bound for Liverpool, but before they left, they played a number of exhibition games — their last opportunity for a tune-up before their European trip. At Hamilton, a team of all-stars from that city and Toronto were no match for them. The score was 61-14. The auditorium was filled with wave after wave of applause. Port Arthur, now Thunder Bay, was captivated with the Grads who were praised not only for their unprecedented basketball skill but also their ladylike behaviour and wholesome character. A Toronto newspaper wrote: "time after time the Grads would sweep down the court three or four abreast, with the ball travelling from one to the other in the most bewildering fashion, oftentime leaving the All-Stars standing in their tracks."

On July 6, the Grads landed at Liverpool. They had eight days in England to relax, act like tourists and sharpen up their basketball. Then it was on to the continent for what was being billed as World Championships. Ten days later, July 16, in a game with the Paris Racing Club, the Grads showed they hadn't lost any of their touch in winning 65-18. Two days later, another Paris team, L'Equipe, was swamped 109-20. Paris newspapers exulted in their opinion that they were seeing the best basketball team in the world. Heading south to Lyons, the Grads were again victorious, 81-9. Nothing seemed to faze the Canadians. France was in the midst of a searing heatwave with temperatures well over 38°C for the outdoor games but still the Grads moved themselves and the ball around to the amazement of the French team. It was a sparkling exhibition of basketball. Moving to Milan, Italy, the Grads had no difficulty in registering a 68-2 score, even though the Italians were a much taller team. In Luxembourg, where the game was played in a steady drizzle and attracted a large turn-out, the Grads won again, 67-6, before a most appreciative audience. In Strasbourg, the Grads played a team which had held them to a 38-7 score in 1924. This time, the Edmonton Girls rolled up 87 points to their 6. Again the reports were approvingly in awe of the team-work and movement of the Canadian girls. The French Magazine *L'Auto*, declared that the Grads were the equal of most men's senior teams and definitely superior to any European women's aggregation.

Continuing in France, the grads defeated a team from Reims, 88-11. In a city best known for Joan of Arc, its basketballers were no match for a team which was rapidly gaining a following throughout all of Europe. Reception after reception was accorded them. Salute followed salute, toast after toast, medal after medal. On August 15, 1928, the Grads defeated another Paris-based team 53-14 in a game billed as the championship of France. Then came the test for the Grads against an all-star aggregation from France for the European and world championship. Outdoors, on a sandy court, the Grads again left no doubt as to their world superiority in posting a 46-14 score. Following yet another banquet and the official awarding of the world title, the Grads, tired but buoyed by their receptions, sailed for home on August 21. Their arrival in Edmonton, on September 3, was the occasion of yet another demonstration of the city's affection for its favourite ambassadors. Shrieking sirens, blaring bands and puttering planes flying overhead were scarcely heard above the frantic cheering of the thousands who lined the parade route. A cacophony of sounds punctuated Edmonton's welcome for its Grads. For Percy Page, Mrs. Page, the team's chaperon, Captain Elsie Bennie, Margaret MacBurney, Kate MacCrae, Mildred MacCormick, Mae Brown, Gladys Frye and

Joan Johnston, it was an unforgettable end to a memorable trip. But all were tired too. It would be six months before the Grads would reconvene to play another game.

When the 1930s brought their gloom and depression to the nation and particularly to the West, the Grads appeared to be a beacon of hope. When their gymnasium facilities were burned forcing them to practise in the normal-school facilities, they made the most of it and continued with their winning ways. The Grads continued to attract international attention. The British magazine *Strength* published an article and photos; the Associated Press carried a story on its wire service throughout the United States; a sporting-goods catalogue from Cincinnati featured the Grads as world champs. James Naismith, the Father of Basketball, as he was known by then, praised the skill and sportsmanship of the Grads and their coach who had a wonderful influence on thousands of people.

Once again, the Grads defended their national title against the Toronto Lakeside team winning the two games 47-17 and 41-27. The four thousand spectators in the stands, as pleased as they were in the Grads gaining another title and beating a team from Toronto in the process, seemed to be looking forward to Underwood Trophy competition. Those games were always emotion charged and thrill packed. In preparation, the Grads decided to begin practising more often with men's intermediate teams so as to sharpen their attack. The Taylor-Trunks were due in Edmonton from Chicago in what promised to be an outstanding series. The Chicago team was taller, had a longer reach and seemed both heavier and stronger. In addition they were reputed to be outstanding sharp-eyed shooters.

And they were every bit as good as their reputation. The first game of the two-game, total-point series was a complete shock to the home-town fans who were accustomed to seeing the Grads' winning ways continue no matter what. It was the first time in seven years that the Grads had lost a game in their home town: the score was a convincing 34-24. Sixty-five hundred followers came to the arena to see with their own eyes not only this team which had defeated their favourites but also to cheer on the locals. The Grads responded by playing as if their lives depended on it. By half-time, the ten-point lead was erased and by the end of the game, much to the delight of the crowd, they had

Los Angeles Olympic Team — the Grads of 1932. Back: Helen Stone, Gladys Fry, J. Percy Page, Elsie Bennie and Edith Stone. Front: Babe Belanger, Mildred McCormack, Margaret MacBurney (Capt.), and Doris Neale.

earned a 64-47 victory. They had retained the championship once again. When called upon to present the trophy, the Chicago coach, also a trustee of the cup play, said that there was no doubt in his mind. It was a simple yet eloquent recognition: "In presenting this trophy to the Grads, I am presenting it to the best basketball team in the world."

There were some who felt that the play of the Grads deteriorated during the next two years. If it had, it probably occurred due to the lack of competition. Teams simply did not want to be so soundly thrashed with so much international exposure attached. On the Grads' 1932 trip to California and the Olympics, they were able to arrange only

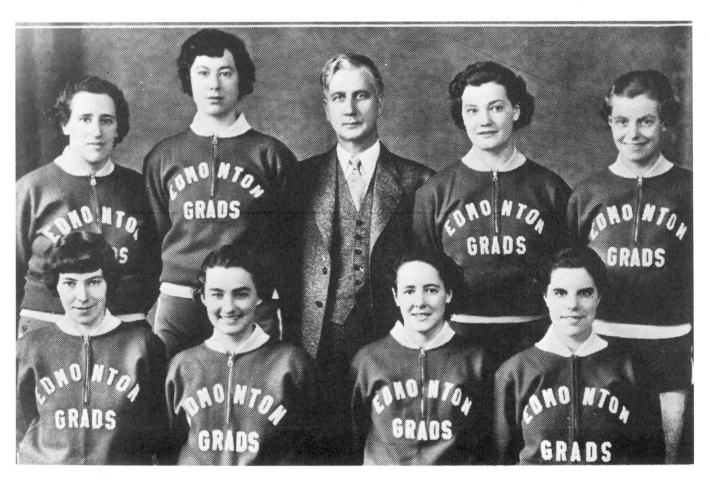

World Champions — the Grads of 1937. Back: Mabel Munton, Noel MacDonald (Capt.), J. Percy Page, Winnie Gallen, Betty Ross. Front: Etta Dann, Helen Northup, Babe Belanger, and Sophie Brown.

three games, hardly worth the problems encountered by the players in arranging for time off from their work. Jobs were hard to find in the Depression years and those who were fortunate to have them wanted to ensure that they kept them. Some were saying, too, that the Grads were simply not as good as they once were, that other teams had caught up to them. Calgary writers, always ready to diminish the flame of anything burning brightly in Edmonton, cited as proof the fact that the Grads had defeated a Calgary team by only thirteen points. But when the Grads defeated the same team by a margin of seventy-eight points, the critics simply stated that it reinforced the notion that the Grads were playing below par most of the time.

In spite of all this, it appeared that none of the Grads' supporters were ready for the 1933 Underwood Series. In June, a three-of-five series, with boys' and girls' rules alternating, was arranged for Edmonton. The opposition was from Durant, Oklahoma. When it was over, the Grads' supporters reacted with stunned disbelief. The Grads had been defeated. All close games, but nonetheless defeated — *in three straight games.* The summer seemed unusually parched that year.

It was a determined group of young athletes who began the 1934 season in the unfamiliar role of former champions. They were a blend of veterans and novices: Margaret McBurney, the captain with eight-years experience, Gladys Fry with seven, Babe Belanger and Noel MacDonald, superb players, while Doris Neale, Helen Stone and Mabel Munton remained steady in their defensive roles. Former captain Elsie Bennie's return after a two-year absence was much welcomed by Page and the team supporters. The season seemed to be a repeat of the 1933 one. In March, a 35-22 victory over Calgary was again taken as a premonition of the hard times which had fallen upon the Grads. With Bennie back in the line-up, her steadying influence greatly felt, the Grads won the Alberta title over Calgary with a 99-21 decision. The Edmonton team had won the right to play for the western title in Vancouver — an easy victory. Again, the Edmonton public seemed to be awaiting American competition; fewer than one thousand came to watch the Grads win their first game against Windsor, 84-24, for the Canadian title.

There was more than a little interest in the Underwood Trophy series of 1934. Basketball was becoming more standardized throughout North America. In the north and eastern United States, men's rules predominated. In the south and west, it was women's rules. Each region had adopted the ten-second rule by this time. The ball now had to be advanced past mid-court within ten seconds or be forfeit. Each region also declared a champion. The Grads, ever looking for new and fresh challenges, decided to challenge the champion of each style. It was the first time that the Amateur Athletic Union of the United States officially sanctioned the series as a bona fide, recognized championship. Previously they had implied, if they had not come right out and said it, that the Grads were playing and defeating inferior competition. This, they said, would be a true test: the real championship of North America.

First were the Chicago Spencer Coals, men's rules champions. Before a large, demonstrative and appreciative audience, the Grads applied the heat to win 100-39. The second game was less of a rout but the Grads had cleared the first hurdle. Then came the Tulsa Stenos, women's rules champions. Physically they appeared to be intimidating being, on the average, two-inches taller than the Grads. They had five players selected as all-Americans. So confident were they that they declared their intention to play men's rules since the Underwood Trophy was thus restricted.

World Champions — the Grads of 1938. Back: Muriel Daniel, Jean Williamson, J. Percy Page, Noel MacDonald (Capt.), Mabel Munton. Front: Sophie Brown, Etta Dann, Helen Northup.

Again, basketball fever gripped Edmonton. The games were all sell-outs. Paramount Pictures arranged to take films to show in movie-houses around the United States and Canada. The Associated Press relayed the news through the wire services. Doubtless, the Americans were disappointed. The Grads again won three straight and once more were making believers of the public on both sides of the border. In 1935, the Tulsa Stenos once again requested the opportunity to challenge. Once again, they were American champions, and once again, the Grads beat them, this time in four games.

By now the Grads had again established themselves and their superiority in North America. Once more, they journeyed to Europe where the 1936 Olympics were being held. While men's basketball was an Olympic sport for the first time (the Canadian team won the silver medal), it was still a demonstration sport for women. And who would be better demonstrators? It was another successful European tour, the Grads winning each of the thirteen games played against various European competitors.

The end of the 1936 tour seemed to be a good time for three of the fifteen Grads to retire. Gladys Frye Douglas, Doris Neale and Babe Belanger reluctantly decided that they had to move on to other matters. Coincidentally, the Grads announced that they would conduct try-outs for aspirants to the world-famous team. Ninety hopefuls showed up at the appointed time on September 10. Once the ninety were pared to twenty-five by the coaches, two replacements

Noel MacDonald, centre 1933-39, perhaps the most skilled of all the Grads.

were selected. Winnie Gallen and Betty Ross were chosen by secret ballots cast by the Grads, Gradettes and the three coaches.

The Grads were more than just a good basketball team to the Edmonton community. They were civic leaders. One was likely to find them raising money for needy families at Christmas, attending opening ceremonies of recreation facilities, offering to stage track-and-field competitions and training young girls in a variety of sports. But across Canada, it was obvious that they were indeed recognized for what they were, a superlative basketball team. In a year-end poll, the Canadian sports writers selected the Grads and the Sarnia Imperials, who were the Grey Cup champions, to tie as the Canadian teams of the year. The irrepressible Grads had rolled on with victory after victory, again winning provincial and national honours as well as successful Underwood defences against Cleveland, Wichita and Tulsa. One wag wrote:

What a game — amidst the thunder
As the Grads went out to plunder
Darting, flashing, checking, scoring:
Seizing, clinging, demon squids;
Sweet co-ordinating passing,
Every Grad her check outclassing,
CHAMPIONS — Percy Page's Kids!!

As the late '30s came to a close, there were a number of difficult decisions the Grads were forced to make. The harsh economic times made each proposed trip the subject of intense scrutiny. Page had always been a relatively democratic coach, involving the girls as much as possible in the decision-making process of who should start and be part of the team. In return, he asked for very little in the way of rules and regulations. There was to be no drinking, no smoking nor any dating on road trips. His stature with the team was such that his wishes were respected at all times. Page, too, was a man with different facets of his life competing for his time. He had his family life, his team; he was a high-school principal and a much sought-after member of the Alberta legislature. There were days when he didn't seem to have enough hours to accomplish all he wanted to do.

In addition, basketball was not a static game. There were continual refinements and changes. During the 1938 season, the jump-ball after each basket was eliminated. Teams could now advance the ball up the court after having been scored upon. It was a change which should have benefited the smaller Grads but one which also meant new teaching and learning for those occasions when the players were closely guarded. Changes or no changes, however, the Grads continued to roll on with another Canadian title, more successful defences of the Underwood Trophy against Chicago and Cleveland teams, all the while maintaining a 37.7 per cent shooting average for the year.

But all good things must come to an end. For a variety of reasons, the Grads decided that the 1939/40 season would be their last. There had always been rumours of such an eventuality but they had never materialized.

But this time, even with the commencement of the Second World War, the Grads' decision was a major topic in Edmonton. After all, they still appeared to be in their prime. They had shocked a team from Des Moines, champions of Iowa, by a 61-20 score. It was obvious to all that they were still on top. While the Grads were preparing for a September series with Wichita, there were more rumours of the disbanding. Anxious supporters from Hardisty sent a petition of 116 names to the team. Many who had signed were among regular supporters who drove the nearly two hundred miles to watch each Grads game. The Grads were touched.

Their next international series was in October, versus Wichita; a series which marked the end of the careers of Captain Noel MacDonald and Mabel Munton. Again, the Grads won three straight, and Percy Page told the twenty-five hundred in attendance that he knew not what the future held in store but that the Grads would probably retire in the spring. In an emotional and appreciative gesture, former Grad Daisy Johnson presented Noel MacDonald and Mabel Munton with heaping baskets of chrysanthemums much to the demonstrated delight of those who had witnessed yet another successful defence of the Underwood Trophy.

Finally, much to the dismay of all, J. Percy Page announced in April of 1940 that, due to the pressures of time, the Grads would cease operations on June 6, 1940 — their silver anniversary. The motion to withdraw was made by Captain Etta Dunn of the present Grads, and Daisy Johnson, a former Grad star and president of the club. The girls stated that both the present members as well as the former players were opposed to carrying on the team except under Mr. Page's direction.

And so after twenty-five years of outstanding play, the Edmonton Grads prepared to play their last series. It promised to be an emotional binge. Their opponents were the Chicago Queen Anne Aces, a team which they had met many times. Edmonton City Council passed a resolution of appreciation commending the Grads for the honours brought to the city by virtue of "their unprecedented record in the world of amateur sport."

Former Grads began to make their way back to Edmonton to watch the twenty-fifth version of the final series. When it began on June 3, 1940, the basketball seemed almost incidental to the wave of nostalgia. When the Grads won the first game, 56-34, it was difficult to believe that the queens of the court could simply call an end to their reign, glorious as it was. Two days later the Grads posted a 45-38 victory to take the second game as well. It was decided that the third game, albeit unnecessary for the championship, would be played in order to allow the public to pay their last tribute to the twenty-five years of championship play.

June 6 was an emotional evening in the Edmonton arena. Gone were any worries of war. Forgotten, momentarily, were any heartaches among the sixty-two hundred

Noel MacDonald, Captain 1938.

witnesses and the countless thousands tuned in by radio. It was only right that the Grads should win the 524th out of 548 played, this one by a 62-52 score. Photographers of all descriptions flooded the perimeter of the court, each one hoping to record some moment for posterity. The followers of the Grads had eagerly filled in ballots to name their favourites over the past twenty-five years. Memories danced before the huge throng's eyes as familiar names were heard in a roll-call of magical honour. Noel MacDonald, first; Etta Dunn, second; Margaret McBurney, third; Gladys Fry, Babe Belanger, Mabel Munton, Elsie Bennie,

Helen Northrup, Millie McCormack, Connie Smith. When the former Grads were also introduced, remarkably, only three were not present. The former players seemed to be enjoying each other's company as much as the spectators did.

At a special banquet held on June 7 at the Corona Hotel, there was hardly a dry eye in the house as the Underwood Trophy was symbolically presented to the first captain of the Grads, Winnie Martin Tait. The twenty-five-year period of the Grads had been linked together beautifully. And Percy Page? The recipient of a beautiful painting

Gathering of the clan — Grad reunion, June 6, 1940.

from his princesses was overcome with emotion. But then, so were each of the 1940 Grads when they were the recipients of specially designed silver spoons, and bouquets of red roses.

Not bad, eh?

Watt's Song

No broken army in retreat,
No loafers, through success gone soft,
But lithe and firm upon their feet.
They have the field with flags aloft.
The game is played, the records stand
The brightest team that ever shone.
Has heard Dismiss! But o'er the land
The spirit of The Gang sweeps on.

Forever changing, yet unchanged,
Tradition linking year by year,
They met the best the world could range —
The best that brought no lasting peer.
Yet if the secret's to be found
In human hearts, 'tis wise to look;
That perfect system isn't bound
Between the covers of a book.

They brought their city more than fame;
They brought their nation more than pride;
The strongest foe, the toughest game,
Were things they simply took in stride,
For first they faced the inward jars —
The jealousy, the selfish dreams;
Those things which make outstanding stars
But wreck consistent winning teams.

The pass that meant another's score.
The faith that fed another's drive
Were constant on and off the floor.
For every year of twenty-five.
Today we face a greater game.
For life and freedom must we play.
And we shall need the gallant flame
The Grads have lit along the way.

Source: The Edmonton Journal *(June 1940).*

99

Nations May Totter

Nations may totter and Politicians Rave
GREAT ISSUES may hang in the Balance
And Even the End of the World may be
   in sight
But what does it matter —
The GRADS ARE PLAYING TONIGHT.

What a game — amidst the thunder
As the Grads went out for plunder

Darting, Flashing, Checking, Scoring,
Seizing, Clinging, Demon Squids,
Sweet co-ordinating passing,
Every Grad her check outclassing
Champions — Percy Page's Kids.

Source: The Edmonton Journal (1 June 1935).

100

The Grads

You may talk about Joe Louis
  Or Perry over seas,
Of Winnipeg's imported stars
  And others such as these;
But when you speak of champions
  Of this or any age,
You'll name the Grads of Edmonton
  And Mr. Percy Page.

There's Helen the Giant Killer.
  And Etta, full of fight,
There's Mabel, the Giant Spiller,
  And Babe who's fast but light.
There's Glad and Doris, the old guards,
  All smeared with scars and fame;

Now face to face meet Noel the Ace,
  The finest in the game.

Today we bid you welcome,
  To join us at our lunch;
We've entertained celebrities,
  But ne'er so fine a bunch.
And now you're going overseas,
  In far-off lands to roam;
We'll miss you when you're far away,
  We'll welcome you back home.

Source: The Edmonton Journal *(5 June 1936)*.

"Tyger! Tyger! Burning Bright . . ."

European skiers, particularly from France, Austria and Switzerland, have always been considered to be the best, perhaps because of their fabled Alps. Without doubt, when Serge Lang, a ski writer for France's *L'Equipe*, advanced the idea of a World Cup to decide the world's best skier, he was thinking of settling the perennial argument of who had the best skiers, the French, the Swiss or the Austrians. Little did he know that the best in the world would come from a land far removed from Europe's Alps, in a country far across the Atlantic, in a province bordering on the Pacific Ocean. That country was Canada; the skier was Nancy Greene.

Lang advanced the notion that a series of nine internationally sanctioned races should be held for both men and women. At each meet there was to be a giant slalom, a special slalom and a downhill race. Points would be awarded on the basis of the first ten finishes, twenty-five for first down to one for tenth. In order to encourage all-around ability, a maximum of seventy-five points could be gained in each area; therefore, the most a competitor could gain from the nine races was two hundred and twenty-five points.

Canadian skiers had never been prominent on the international ski circuit. The men, particularly, were behind the women, who, at least, did have two impressive placings in the past. Lucille Wheeler had won a bronze medal at the Cortina D'Ampezzo 1956 Winter Olympics, it being earned in the downhill event. Anne Heggtveit was a gold medalist in 1960 at the Squaw Valley Olympics. But in 1967 and 1968, Canada was looked upon as being the home of skiing champions. It was a time for centennial celebrations, the year of Expo. It was the year that Canada, in the person of Nancy Greene, would be recognized throughout the world for its skiing prowess.

Nancy Green was born in Ottawa, May 11, 1943, but it was in Rossland, British Columbia, where the young Nancy learned her skiing after the family moved there. At sixteen, she was a member of Canada's National Ski Team, a costly avocation since members of the fledgeling group were responsible for their own expenses. Nancy had a good relationship with the citizens of the small B.C. town. So much so that the Rossland Mountain Ski Club contributed to her support. On at least two occasions — in

1961 when she needed funds for a year of practise in Europe and in 1962 at the World Championships — Rossland residents raised some two thousand dollars to see her through. All were quite confident that the determined young skier would pay many returns on their investment.

And in time, she would. But the course wasn't always smooth. Skiing was not a sport which had great public support in Canada; the Canadian ski team of 1959 had been described as a ragtag organization with feckless moral support and little financial backing. The seventeen-year-old Nancy had placed twenty-second in the downhill at the Squaw Valley 1960 Olympics. By the 1962 world championships, she had worked her way to a creditable fifth in the same event, in spite of some very real shortcomings in the program. The lack of financial support, combined with internal problems of the ski team, caused Nancy to train with the men's team for the next two years. She seemed to thrive. During the 1965 season, various European ski resorts, and reports, buzzed with excitement as she constantly placed in the top five while winning four events, coming in with second places in four others. A virtual unknown in her own country, Nancy Greene was attracting much notice in Europe. The 1966 season continued in the same manner until the last race of the season in Portillo, Chile. There in August, a disappointed Nancy Greene, her pole taped to an injured arm, raced to a fourth in the giant slalom and fell in the downhill as well as the special slalom.

But Nancy Greene wasn't one to quit in adversity, although occasionally tears might flow because of some disappointment. She had worked too hard and trained too long. When she was six years old, speeding down the steepest part of Red Mountain in Rossland, tethered by a rope held by her father, she had learned to conquer fear. The skiing season capped her year-round regimen of bicycling and running or willingly carrying her younger brother up the stairs to bed, knowing that she was building up her strength in the process. It seemed as if every waking moment was geared towards becoming the best; 1967 was to demonstrate, vividly, that she had made it.

During the first year of the World Cup competitions, speculation among the European nations suggested that France, because of Marielle Goitschel and Annie Famose, or perhaps Austria because of Erika Schinegger, would run away with the competition, thus settling all of the arguments as to who was the best. Very seldom were North American skiers, in general, or Nancy Greene, in particular, mentioned in the same analysis of the situation.

Yet, when the season began in January, the Europeans were shocked into disbelief. Nancy Greene had exploded into prominence with four consecutive victories! From Canada came numerous congratulatory messages from suddenly awakened citizens from all walks of life. Even the Governor General sent along his praises. European ski capitals were incredulous — but unconvinced. Male skiing champion, Jean Claude Killy, of France, paid Nancy a compliment of sorts by attributing her success to her attacking the course instead of concentrating on *le style*. On this side of the Atlantic, however, Nancy was causing many to take notice. American publications such as *Newsweek* and *Sports Illustrated* began to follow this "friendly but frank . . . fiery competitor who will yell and slam her poles into the snow and weep at any racing disappointment."

It was with even more disbelief that the Europeans learned that Nancy Greene would be leaving the ski circuit temporarily to compete in Canada. True, she was leading with 126 points to Annie Famose's 95 and Marielle Goitschel's 90 but that didn't seem like enough reason to leave in the middle of the circuit. There were still three meets in France and Italy. Many were convinced that her absence would cost her what seemed to be a certain title if she stayed, but Nancy didn't appear to be overly concerned about that. She wanted to give the younger skiers in Canada a taste of high-level competition. Her presence on the ski slopes at home would also provide a much needed boost to the ski program. The price that she might pay was the title, but she hoped to offset that by providing her own presence at the Canadian races. Nancy left the tour for six weeks while her rivals continued to harvest valuable World Cup points.

When Nancy rejoined the World Cup circuit's North American leg at Franconia, New Hampshire, it was obvious that her instinct and reflexes had suffered from the lack of intensive competition. Her best showing was a third in the giant slalom. Her opponents had placed higher, so that in the standings Goitschel was now first with 169 points, Famose was second with 146 while Nancy Greene was now in third place with 141 points.

There wasn't much time to return to peak performance nor was there much hope of catching the leader, but there was a chance! At Vail, Colorado, in deteriorating ski conditions, Nancy came first in the giant slalom and second in downhill. She had picked up ten points giving her 151 to her second-place rival's 158 and Marielle Goitschel's 169. There was only one more race to go — at Jackson's Hole, Wyoming.

Nancy Green's challenge was clear and simple. She had to win all three races on the program. Not that she would gain any more points from doing that. The only race that would give her enough points was the slalom. She had forty points and therefore could benefit from a victory to the maximum of twenty-five points. Both of her major competitors had seventy points in the event and therefore could gain only a maximum of five. Nancy had to win in order to get maximum points, at the same time preventing the opponents from gaining theirs. On the surface it appeared possible — but highly improbable. It was a tall order — some said impossible. Perhaps for most, but for the plucky Canadian, who was beginning to be known to her team-mates as Tiger, it was an opportunity to go all out. The first indication of what might happen was when Nancy Greene won both runs of the twelve-hundred-metre giant slalom and downhill. It added nothing to her totals but managed to keep her opponents in reach. Only the slalom was left now, the last race of the season.

After the first run, Nancy Greene was in second place, .04 seconds ahead of Marielle Goitschel in third place. It was icy on the fifty-six-gate course. It was icy even though some parts were slushy due to the fresh falling snow that Sunday morning. It was as if the winter was relaxing its grip, giving way to spring. It was March 26, 1967.

The race organizers could not have planned it any better. Third on the course was Nancy; her two competitors were immediately behind her. They at least would have the advantage of knowing what Nancy had done. She would have to shoot for the imaginary time. With a strong forward leap, she bolted onto the straightaway gaining speed with each thrust of the poles. Into the wide turn, followed by a tight sharp pattern of ins and outs she took each gate instinctively knowing when to commit herself. As she came out of the last gate, again her poles meshed to increase her speed across the finish line . . . 44.51 giving her a combined time of 90.67. Now, she could only wait.

Next was Marielle Goitschel: she needed a time of at least 44.46. As Nancy Greene watched, her competitor skied flawlessly through each gate and across the finish line. Nancy's heart sank. She waited for the time

to be flashed on the scoreboard. It was 43.35 but then, in an instant, changed to 44.53. The Tiger was still ahead by .07 seconds! Marielle Goitschel made her way to Nancy's side to give her a big hug. Both now turned to watch Florence Steurer. When her time of 46.91 was posted, the impossible had been done. Nancy Greene had won the slalom and with it the World Cup! She earned a total of 176 points to Marielle Goitschel's 172 and Annie Famose's 158. Nancy Greene, the unheralded young skier from an unheralded skiing country, was the best woman skier in the world!

But was it a fluke? Many of the Europeans thought so and they seemed determined to prove it during the next season when a new World Cup would be sought after, as well as the Olympic crown.

Nancy Greene could have been excused if she chose to bask in the glory of the public praise and accolades which she received on her return home. After all, especially in centennial year when nationalism was rampant everywhere in Canada, she was a genuine national hero and much in demand. She maintained a whirlwind pace, all the while attempting to keep herself in good condition in spite of her many public appearances. The Government of Canada, recognizing her high level of accomplishment, asked her to be a member of a three-person committee to investigate and make recommendations about the state of sport in Canada. She willingly obliged, bringing the perspective of a highly gifted athlete to the deliberations. In the back of

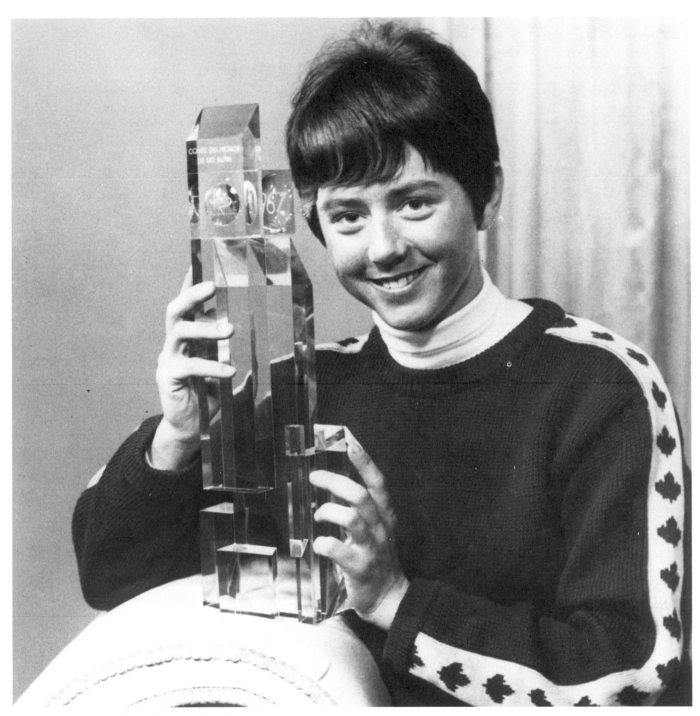

Nancy Greene, the Tiger of the slopes.

her mind always, however, was the thought that another season would arrive shortly and she had to be ready to demonstrate her expertise once again.

And so, in January 1968, the time arrived for another series of World Cup races, only now with the pressure augmented by the Winter Olympics to he held in Grenoble, France, right in the Europeans' backyard. The jungle of competition was becoming even more tortuous for the young Tiger. After the first two events of the new season, Nancy was in third place with 30 points behind Austria's Gerraud Gabl with 48 points and Marielle Goitschel's 40. All seemed to be proceeding fairly smoothly when sudden misfortune, both mental and physical, struck. While training at Badgastein, Austria, for the Olympics, the defending champion fell, tearing her ankle ligaments as a result. The next two weeks saw the inactive Nancy slide from third to sixth place in the standings. Then, some two weeks later, her misfortunes were compounded when the International Olympic Committee lodged a charge of professionalism against Nancy saying that she had received a five-thousand-dollar scholarship from Notre Dame in Nelson, B.C. For some time, it appeared as if she might not be able to compete even if her ankle did heal in time. Soon, it was shown that she did not receive the scholarship; her amateur status was protected. She could compete in the Olympics, providing that her ankle could be rehabilitated.

At Saint-Gervais, France, in an attempt to test her ankle in competition but with as little twisting and turning as possible, Nancy Greene came twenty-fourth in a field of sixty in the downhill. French skier Isabelle Mir was first. More rehabilitation was necessary. The Olympics were important, not only in themselves, but also in that they counted towards the standings in the World Cup.

At the opening ceremonies, February 6, 1968, Nancy Greene led the Canadian contingent of athletes and officials who marched behind the flag she proudly carried. At twenty-four, she was the veteran of the team which included Betsy Clifford, fifteen, from Ottawa, Judi Leinweber, seventeen, from Nelson, B.C., and Karen Dokka, twenty-one, from Burnaby, B.C. When the blustery weather allowed for the downhill to take place, it was a dejected Nancy Greene who walked slowly back to the athletes' quarters. She had come tenth. For one-half hour afterwards, she fought tears. It was even more discouraging since she had posted the fastest practice time the day before.

But the disappointment had to be forgotten. The slalom was next. Her ankle had held up fairly well and now she had another chance. With renewed confidence, Nancy wove her way through the course towards the finish line. Second! A silver medal! She was only .29 seconds behind Marielle Goitschell. Even though it was in itself quite an accomplishment and only the third medal ever won by a Canadian at the Olympics in skiing, she knew that she could do better. She would do better! She wanted the gold! And she would have it, or fall in the attempt!

On February 15, 1968, the flying Tiger won the gold medal in the Olympic giant slalom. Of forty-eight skiers from eighteen nations, racing through sixty-eight gates, Nancy Greene finished an outstanding 2.63 seconds ahead of her nearest rival. Through Nancy's head flashed memories of the promise she had made to herself as a sixteen-year-old: seeing Anne Heggtveit win her gold medal in the same event in 1960, she had made a commitment to herself that she too would win an Olympic gold medal. And now, she had one to go with her silver!

Amid all of the euphoria and celebrations both in Canada and among the Canadian contingent at the Olympics, Nancy sought to refocus her thoughts and effort on the still-continuing World Cup circuit. She couldn't afford to spend much time basking in any glory. Now, as a result of her strong Olympic showing, she had moved up to fifth place. When she continued the circuit and placed first at Chamonix, she assumed the lead with a total of 101 points. It was a slim hold on the title but enough to renew her confidence.

But now, as if nothing came easy to Nancy, other matters vied for her attention. She had April examinations at Notre Dame. As well, grateful Canadians wanted to pay homage to the queen of the slopes. She returned to Canada on February 27 for these reasons and also to prepare for the remaining races to be held in North America. By the time the American international meet was held March 22-24, at Sun Valley, Idaho, the Tiger's performances were such that she won the downhill slalom, the giant slalom and the combined yet could obtain no points for her World Cup total.

On March 26, Nancy announced her intention to retire at the end of the season, saying: "After competing eleven months a year for ten years, it's time . . . for some personal life . . . If you're going to quit, you might as well do it now when you're ahead. This is the most opportune time. This year, I had set gold medals and world championships as my goals. With those behind me, it seems that to set these goals again would be no progress at all."

Nancy Tiger Greene's final international race took place at Heavenly Valley, South Lake Tahoe, California. She had a fifth in the giant slalom and a second in the slalom. Her total points for the year were a leading 191, ten more than her 1967 total; thirty-two more than second-place Isabelle Mir and thirty-eight more than third-place, Florence Steurer. The Tiger could retire burning bright.

The title was taken from "The Tyger" from Songs of Experience by William Blake.

Canadian Ski Song

*The hills lie white and silent sleeping in the
    snow,*
*The trail lies tracked before us, tramped by
    other skis,*
The sky is blue above us, urging us to go
*And glide the mantled meadows, breast the
    upland breeze.*
*The Sumac cones glow crimson, red against
    the white,*
*A Blue-Jay blue and brilliant screams across
    the trail,*
*The snow beneath us crunches, faster grows
    our flight,*
As swiftly o'er waters glide the ships full-sail.
The energy of freedom fills the veins with fire
*The heart beats fast untrammeled, free as
    clouds that race*
*We climb and glide the uplands, found the
    heart's desire,*
*The rush of air around us, the wind against
    the face.*

*The iron hills surround us, solemn in their
    sleep,*
*The susurrus of swishing skis fills the
    atmosphere,*
*As rhythmically gliding, swift where slopes
    are steep*
*We rush the narrow speedway, dropping
    sudden, sheer.*
*The ancient and eternal lure of snow and
    hill,*
Now calls and ever will call, stir out lethargy,
*Until we glide the ski-trail free of heart and
    will,*
*Free of the earth's great uplands, free as the
    winds are free.*

Arthur S. Bourinot

Source: Carvin, J., editor, Canadian Poets
*(Toronto: McClelland and Stewart Ltd.,
1930).*

The Song of the Ski

Norse am I when the first snow falls;
Norse am I till the ice departs
The fare for which my spirit calls
Is blood from a hundred viking-hearts.
The curved wind wraps me like a cloak;
The pines blow out their ghostly smoke.
I'm high on the hill and ready to go —
A wingless bird in a world of snow:
Yet I'll ride the air
With a dauntless dare
that only a child of the north can know.

The bravest ski has a cautious heart
And moves like a tortoise at the start,
But when it tastes the tang of the air
It leaps away like a frightened hare.
The day is gloomy, the curtains half-drawn,
And light is stunted as at the dawn:
But my foot is sure and my arm is brawn.

I poise on the hill and I wave adieu:
(My curving skis are firm and true)
The slim wood quickens, the air takes fire
And sings to me like a gypsy's lyre.
Swifter and swifter grows my flight;
The dark pines ease the unending white.

The lean, cold birches, as I go by,
Are like blurred etchings against the sky.

One am I for a moment's joy
With the falling star and the plunging bird.
The world is swift as an Arab boy;
The world is sweet as a woman's word.
Never came such a pure delight
To a bacchanal or a sybarite:
Swifter and swifter grows my flight,
And glad am I, as I near the leap,
That the snow is fresh and the banks are
   deep.

Swifter and swifter on I fare,
And soon I'll float with the birds on air,
The speed is blinding; I'm over the ridge,
Spanning space on a phantom bridge.
The drifts await me; I float, I fall:
The world leaps up like a lunging carp.
I land erect and tired winds drawl
A lazy tune on a broken harp.

Child of the roofless world am I;
Not of those hibernating drones
Who fear the grey of a wintry sky

And the shrieking wind's ironic tones,
Who shuffle cards in a cloud of smoke
Or crawl like frozen flies at chess,
Or gossip all day with meddling folk
In collar of starch and a choking dress.
Come, ye maids of the vanity-box,
Come, ye men of the stifling air;
The white wind waits at your door and
    knocks;
The white snow calls you everywhere.
Come, ye lads of the lounge and chair,
And gird your feet with the valiant skis
And mount the steed of the winter air
And hold the reins of the winter breeze.,

Lord of the mountains dark with pine!
Lord of the fields of smoking snow!
Grant this vagrant heart of mine
A path of wood where my feet may go,
And a roofless world to my journey's end,
And a cask of wind for my cup of wine,
And yellow gold of the sun to spend,
And at night the stars in endless line,
And, after it all, the hand of a friend —
The hand of a trusted friend in mine.

Wilson MacDonald

Source: New Horizons (Toronto:
McClelland & Stewart, Ltd.).

Kathy Kreiner, Queen of the Hill, Gold Medallist 1976.

Queen of the Hill

Kathy Kreiner, today is the day,
You can look at the world, and be able to
  say.
Only with will power, courage and skill,
Am I able to say, I am queen of the hill.

Though the battle was long, the climb was
  rough,
You proved to the world, no matter how
  tough
The going would be, with the courage and
  will,
You'd prove to the world you are queen of
  the hill.

From the Porcupine hills, to the Alpine
  slope,
From a childhood dream, to a teenage hope.
Through spills and losses, you still had the
  will,
To prove to the world, you are queen of the
  hill.

Though the losses were tough, the battle a
  strain,
You picked yourself up and tried it again.
For only through losses, can one gain the
  skill,
To reach for the top, to be queen of the hill.

Yes, Kathy Kreiner, the day, the day of all
  days,
To remember the ones who helped long the
  way.
And pass on, to others, wherever you will,
The hope and the courage, to be the queen
  of the hill.

Gerry Straatman

Source: The Daily Press, *Timmons, Ont.*
(16 February 1976).

Slalom Hill

This is the slalom hill
Pennants of yellow and red
flutter and startle the snow
where skiers flow
in rapid, rhythmic turns
about the poles.

Swift prows of far-off ships
the skis cloud their track
and the sneer of the snow
curls to a misty wake
where they veer and tack,
zig-zag, flag to flag,
then the final plunge,
the ultimate lunge,
to the edge of the crowd below.
The tow of rope,
festooned with festive sweaters,
slacks and snoods,
drags its slow length up the slope
through the woods,
disgorging its load at the top,

the eternal circle
of life itself,
turning, turning,
life renewed,
turning, turning
so it goes,
the steady flow,
all day long,
of restive youth
thronging, thronging,
up and down,
up and down,
thronging, thronging,
they never stop;
nothing is ever still
on the slalom hill.

Arthur S. Bourinot

Source: Watcher of Men, The Selected
Poems of Arthus S. Bourinot (1947-1966)
(Toronto, 1966).

Golfers

Like Sieur Montaingne's distinction
between virtue and innocence
what gets you is their unbewilderment

They come into the picture suddenly
like unfinished houses, gapes and planed
wood dominating a landscape

And you see at a glance
among sportsmen they are the
metaphysicians intent, untalkative,
pursuing Unity

(What finally gets you is their chastity)

And that no theory of pessimism is complete
which altogether ignores them

Irving Layton

Source: The Darkening Fire, Selected
Poems, 1945-1968

Lacrosse: The Sport of Canada

*I'm one of the old lacrosse boys; a friend of
   the gutted stick,*
*I tell you the old game's got me; at times I
   think I'm sick*
*Of the days it takes for training; of the
   games that are earned and lost,*
*"I'm through," I say, when we put away our
   sticks with the autumn frost.*
*But when May comes down on the West
   Wind, 'tis then that I feel the pang*
*At the thought of the fun I'd be missing, and
   you find me back with the gang.*

*I've done my stint in the scorching heat; a
   heat that no one knows,*
*Who has not lived for a Summer in "Our
   Lady of the Snows."*
*I've felt the grass a-sizzle, and I've felt my
   tongue hang out;*

*While the sweat on my neck and forehead,
   streamed down like a water-spout.*
*I've seen the field a-whirling, and never
   really knew*
*How I nerved myself for another sprint, and
   stayed till the whistle blew.*

*There are jolts and you bet you feel them,
   when you get the body fair —*
*Some bumps you take, and some bumps
   you give — in the end you call it square.*
*Maybe you shed a tooth or two; you skin is
   not always whole.*
*But it's worth it when you grab the ball, and
   bang in the winning goal.*
*You know the crowd is with you; you can
   hear the loud-mouthed fan;*
*"Go down on the home, for the love of
   Mike," or "Everybody cover a man."*

And, oh, your blood goes leaping, when the
*   boys in the bleachers roar;*
"Bore in on the nets, break the tie — just
*   two minutes to score."*
You have pulled out a game by a hair's breath,
*   or you've cracked beneath the strain;*
But they still have a thrill, in after years,
*   when you play them all over again.*

So measure the creases ready, and put the
*   nets in place;*
The teams are padded and steady, and the
*   ball is there to face.*
I'll be out to do my darndest, if I'm only an
*   "also ran."*
For this is the sport of Canada — a game
*   that takes a man.*

Fred Jacob

The Loser's Wail

*How confident the fighter is the day before
the scrap,*
*While signs of glowing health are seen upon
his battered map,*
*He is frisky as a lamb that gambols in its
glee,*
*I never was in better shape, in all my life
says he,*
*But when he has received his bumps he tells
another tale,*
*He beats it to the sporting ed. and wails a
woeful wail,*
*I hadn't ought to fought, he says I had a
case of grippe,*

*I also had the measles and a bad attack of
pip;*
*I broke a pair of knuckles on my sparring
partner's head,*
*Instead of being in the ring I ought to have
been in bed;*
*I had the worse attack of gout a fellow ever
saw,*
*But even then the worst they should have
gave me was a draw.*

George Phair

Source: Sun, *Vancouver (26 March 1914).*

The Stanley Cup and 1896

The Stanley Cup. The mention of it today conjures up images of the best teams in the National Hockey League, representing cities thousands of kilometres apart in Canada and the United States, their teams exhibiting speed, balance, alertness, quickness while all the time under the threat of body contact. Lord Stanley probably didn't know what he was starting when he gave his famous hockey trophy for supremacy away back in 1892. The game was young back then, very much in its infancy with different parts of the country playing by different sets of rules. When the Cup became a much sought-after symbol, its status was such that uniformity of rules followed.

Lord Stanley of Preston, the sixteenth Earl of Derby, became Canada's Governor General in 1888. He developed into such an avid follower of hockey that he founded a team: outfitted in blazing red sweaters, the Rebels from Rideau Hall. Home games were played on an open-air rink at Government House and Stanley's sons were integral members. But it was Stanley's favourite team, the Ottawas, later to be known as the Silver Seven, that captured his fancy. Whenever clubs from Toronto or Montreal issued challenges to the Ottawas, the games were eagerly anticipated. Wherever hockey fans gathered, arguments raged long into the night as to which team was the best in the land. Lord Stanley thought he had a solution. At a banquet for the Ottawa club, the following letter was read:

> *March 18, 1892.*
> *I have for some time been thinking it would be a good thing if there was a challenge cup which should be held from year to year by the champion hockey team in the Dominion. There does not appear to be any such outward and visible sign of championship at present and considering the general interest which the matches now elicit and importance of having the game played fairly and under rules generally recognized, I am willing to give a cup which shall be held from year to year by the winning team.*
> *I am not quite certain that the present regulations governing the arrangements of matches give entire satisfaction and it would be worth considering whether they could not be arranged so that each team would play once at home and once at the place that their opponents hail from.*

And so a large silver bowl, purchased in England for ten guineas (about fifty dollars), became what has been called the most cherished possession in Canadian sport.

But what was hockey like in the 1890s? For one thing, a game was complete when one team scored a goal. A set time for play did not come about until clubs became dependent on spectators for revenue and therefore it became necessary to advertise a definite time of play. Two halves of forty to forty-five minutes each became the norm. Teams had a seventh player, the rover. Passing could only occur behind the puck carrier — that is, it had to be onside. Boards enveloped the ice but they could range in height anywhere from fifteen centimetres to one metre. At first a hard lacrosse ball was used but when it bounced uncontrollably, sometimes into the stands or through the windows, an enterprising person cut the top and bottom off, thus producing a flat disc — the forerunner of the puck. Of course, the ice was natural and therefore at the mercy of the elements whether it was located indoors or outdoors. Skates were fastened to one's shoes by a screw or clamps; sticks were a cross between the field-hockey type and the modern variety, the former fading from general use as the puck became universally adopted.

But to return to the Stanley Cup. There have been many classic series played for the venerable trophy. One was in 1896, when a team from Winnipeg, the Victorias, challenged the Montreal team, also known as the Victorias. Montreal was the current Stanley Cup holder. Manitoba was a recent arrival into Confederation (1870); its capital city of Winnipeg had a thriving population of thirty thousand. The huge influx from Europe had not yet begun; Manitoba was very English and influenced much by Ontario. British settlement prevailed, hence the name Victorias for the western team. It also explained the name of the Montreal team since it represented the English toe-hold in the province of Quebec.

The Stanley Cup had been a challenge trophy from its inception. Any team could challenge the holder to play a game or series of games for it. Two trustees from Ottawa, P.D. Ross and Sheriff Sweetland, had the final say in whose challenge was to be accepted. In some years it was hectic since there were so many intangibles: weather, ice availability, travel, loss of time from jobs. Beginning in 1896, there was an attempt made to place the competitions on a more orderly basis. The Ontario, Quebec and Manitoba hockey associations agreed to rotate challenges between the non-champion associations. This year, 1896, it was Manitoba's turn. Their representatives would play the Cup holders who were from Quebec. The winners would be allowed to defend the Cup on their own home rink.

The one game for the 1896 Stanley Cup was set for February 14, in Montreal. It was to be a renewal of sorts. Anxious to test their team against acknowledged top competition, the Winnipeg team had played an exhibition with Montreal the previous year. They lost, but they hoped to demonstrate that they had

Lord Stanley donated the Stanley Cup at a dinner March 18, 1892.

learned their lessons well in their effort to become the first team to return west with the Stanley Cup.

There were three rinks in Winnipeg in 1896, each dependent upon the weather, each well used by the public. Hockey was popular: there were senior, intermediate, junior and a variety of recreational leagues in existence. In senior, a resurgence was taking place because of the residence rule in vogue: players had to reside in the geographical area the team represented and the residence had to be for a certain period of time. Preparations for the trip to Montreal began in earnest in the new year. Until then, the Winnipeg team had a very limited schedule. Only one game had been played, that on December 21. It had been a disputed contest with the other senior hockey team in town, the Winnipegs. On that occasion, the Victorias lost, but in the rematch on January 9, the Vics gained a 4-0 victory.

The city was optimistic. Because the game would be played in February, it meant that the western city would have a full month to prepare. As well, their team was essentially the same as the year before. Merritt had replaced Shepherd in goal and the 'Peg was abuzz with his aggressive goal-tending since he had taken to wearing cricket pads in the nets. Nobody else was doing it and since it wasn't barred by the rules, he continued to wear them and thrilled the spectators with each booming stop. The rest of the team was solid: Flett was at point; Higginbotham at cover point; while Bain, Campbell, Howard and Armytage, the forwards, were very

familiar with each other's play and had impressed during their tour of the east in 1895. Even the spare, Benson, from the Victorias' intermediate team, could fit in quite well if needed.

In the meantime, however, the club had some concerns. They still wished to play more games and, as well, needed to raise more money for the expensive trip to Montreal. Armytage, the Captain, was responsible for the team's conditioning and attempted to develop a conscientious system of training by his careful attention. All was aimed at peaking for the February 14th date. By all reckoning they seemed to be on target. On Saturday, January 18, the Victorias defeated their rivals, the Winnipegs, 8-1. A few days later, their improvement was even more obvious; they defeated them this time, 15-4. Victoria supporters were enthusiastically ecstatic. Their garnet-coloured favourites seemed to be everywhere. They had managed to score goals in fifteen, thirty and forty-five seconds. And when the news reached the west that the Ottawa team had defeated Montreal in their own home rink, their optimism continued to grow.

Final preparations, in the form of a benefit, were made on February 4. By then it was obvious that the Winnipegs were no rivals for the strong Vics. It was decided that the most effective results could be gained from pairing the Winnipeg forwards with the Victorias' defence and the Victorias' forwards with the Winnipegs' defence. Not only was the game highly entertaining, it was tactically valuable. It ended in a 2-2 draw. As part of the program intended to attract as many paying spectators as possible, the Victorias' intermediates defeated the Winnipegs' intermediates by a 1-0 score in a game played on snow-shoes. Everybody seemed happy: the Victorias had a thorough, high-tempo work-out; the intermediates gained some nine hundred patrons. Two hundred dollars was presented to the Victorias towards the eight hundred needed for the trip.

On Monday, February 10, 1896, as the 12:20 departure time neared for the CPR train to Montreal, the station, already bubbling with noisy excitement from the hundreds of Victorias' supporters, began to rock with the customary "three cheers and a tiger." There was no doubt that this was a civic mission of great importance. At 12:20, the wondrous sleek locomotive, puffing its black smoke in powerful staccato snorts, its wheels moving steadily onwards, began to pull out of the station. It was a noble crusade. The train, determined and ever moving onward, seemed to personify the approach that the westerners had taken towards their objective. Even the train trip had been well planned, organized and carried out. Captain Armytage continued to supervise the conditioning of his team-mates, encouraging exercise while the train was moving, and walking about during the train stops. When Ottawa was reached, Tuesday, it was an opportunity to stay overnight and visit the House of Commons. Arrival in Montreal on Wednesday would allow two practices before the big match on Friday.

Meanwhile, back in Winnipeg, the *Free Press* eagerly reported all the news: Montreal bettors were eagerly backing their team; Montreal wished a postponement because of injuries to three of its players; Montreal wanted an official from Ottawa to referee the game. The reports irritated the west. It seemed as if Montreal was creating an atmosphere conducive to itself: if it won, it would be in spite of the injuries it had and therefore would be a great victory; if it lost, well . . . it had all those injuries . . . what could be expected? But there was other news: the Winnipeg Vics were much in demand for exhibition games, a request for one coming from Saint John, New Brunswick. It was necessary for the club to make an announcement: if they won the Stanley Cup, they would not play another game in the east but would return home in ten days; if they lost, they would reluctantly embark on a three-week tour of the east to show how good they really were.

In Winnipeg, Friday, February 14, couldn't come fast enough. Hockey was the number-one topic — this in a city where curling was usually the pre-eminent sport. Most planned to be over at the *Free Press* offices where a special set-up would receive telegraphed information from Montreal and post it for all to see, the information spreading like wildfire throughout the crowd.

Meanwhile, back in Montreal, the westerners who headquartered at the Windsor Hotel, were pointed out wherever they went. All of the attention they received helped to give the team a quiet sense of confidence. There was also an attempt to guarantee their good fortune. A porter at the hotel, a burly, jovial man, had joined in the team's camaraderie, taking the players' minds off the game with his good-natured bantering. The players were convinced that he was a good-luck charm. They begged him to accompany them to the rink, buying a ticket for him. The porter stated that he would be glad to come when he could but that he would arrive late and might have to leave early. He promised that he would do his best to be there to cheer on his new-found friends.

On Friday, February 14, 1896, before a full house of two thousand spectators, at 8:45 pm, the Montrealers took to the ice, much to the delight of their followers who gave them prolonged applause. Each movement of every player seemed to be an occasion for yet another round of cheers as the home side went through its warm-ups. A few minutes later, Captain Armytage led the Winnipeg players to the ice, and the twenty-five Winnipeg supporters who had accompanied the team from the west tried to match the exuberance of the overwhelmingly pro-Montreal crowd. The warm-up period continued for fifteen minutes; each western player occasionally searched the stands for their good-luck charm — but to no avail.

At nine o'clock the game began. Umpires Ross and Sterneck, of Winnipeg and Montreal, stationed themselves while Referee Martin of Toronto prepared to drop the puck for the face-off. Montreal's McDougall won the draw and shot the puck into the Winnipeg zone to the cheers of the assembly. Higginbotham, however, promptly lifted it out and back into the Montreal zone. To the delight of the small band of Winnipeg supporters, play stayed in the Montreal area for the next five minutes as the western Victorias covered their opponents with close checking. Ten minutes into the first forty-minute half, the porter arrived and took his seat among the Winnipeg cheering section. As if on cue, Howard took a pass on a wonderful lift by Flett and moved it to Captain Armytage in front of the Montreal goal. The Winnipeg player made no mistake and "placed the disc fairly between the posts." Among the Winnipeg supporters, there was jubilation; the Montrealers sat in stunned silence and only grudgingly gave scattered respectful applause. The first game or goal was Winnipeg's.

Some ten minutes later, Winnipeg scored again. Once more it was Armytage who figured in the play. This time he carried the puck down the ice deftly avoiding all the Montreal team on his solo rush. Circling behind the Montreal net, he attracted the defenders to him whereupon he coolly passed the puck in front of the net to Campbell who scored to make it two games to nil. It was a beautiful goal, all the more so since the Winnipeg team had played short-handed for five minutes when Bain, who had been previously warned, was sent off the ice for playing offside. As the half ended, with the same two-games-to-nothing score, the westerners trooped into the dressing-room to rest up for the second half, a look of quiet confidence and determination on each man's face.

With the recommencement of the game, the western players looked up into the stands. Their good luck porter was gone. The rink was now a noisy enclave. Words of encouragement, loud and sustaining words, were being offered to the home team by their large number of supporters. With passage of

Winnipeg Victorias, first Stanley Cup winners for the West, 1896.

time, play became very close, each player keeping a close mark on his check. Tempers were beginning to flare. At the eight-minute mark, Bain of Winnipeg and Henderson of Montreal were sent off the ice for the duration of the match because of their scuffling. It was now six-man hockey, the extra amount of ice available seemingly making for a much faster game. Each team had to have its wits about it especially when the puck was lifted above the thirty-centimetre boards and into the crowd who

The Stanley Cup as it appeared before changes were made to the base.

threw it back onto the ice, play continuing without a whistle. In the final fifteen minutes, the Montreal team applied great pressure but to no avail. At the end of the second forty minutes the score remained the same, 2-0. Winnipeg was the new Stanley Cup champion!

In the Manitoban capital, there was bedlam and euphoria. As word had spread during the Winnipeg lead, hundreds more supporters made their way to the *Free Press*. Celebrations continued long into the night as the Manitoba, Queen's and Clarendon Hotels became centres for the festivities. City fathers hastily made preparations for a gigantic welcome-home while congratulatory telegrams were being sent to their sons in the east.

Meanwhile, back in Montreal, the victorious Victorias were hosted to a pleasant dinner and reception by the Montreal Victorias' directors and players. It was more dutiful than joyous, though. *The Winnipeg Free Press* reported:

> *alas for the frailty of human hopes. Montreal, tonight, is clothed in sackcloth and ashes and the sports have gone to sleepless beds with empty pocketbooks. The 'peg contingent on the other hand, have enough money to start a private bank. No less than 2,000 gold plunkers were passed over the Windsor counter after the match tonight and went down into the jeans of Winnipeg supporters.*

Plans for the February 24th arrival in Winnipeg were made to welcome the new champions. They would travel by private CPR car stopping *en route* in Toronto, but first a number of details had to be looked after. Winnipeg's share of the gate receipts was the grand total of $133. It had been $135 but two dollars were used to buy extra tickets for supporters, including Howard's mother and the good-luck porter. The Stanley Cup itself had already been presented to Manager Cade. All marvelled at the sight of the trophy they had only read about. It was like a beautiful silver punch-bowl, capable of holding seven litres and made of shining sterling silver. Not to be forgotten in their exuberance, the players had a happy duty to perform; they each contributed to a fund and bought their good-luck porter a beautiful new suit of clothes.

Monday, February 24 was bitterly cold in Winnipeg. Nobody seemed to notice. Preparations to greet the new champions were being enthusiastically made. At the CPR station, thousands were stretching their necks, standing on their toes, straining to get a vantage point as the train carrying their heroes chugged slowly into the terminal. What a sight! The front of the engine was adorned with a giant Union Jack, the cowcatcher serving as a base for hockey sticks and brooms. Some thought that the curlers had to have their say but others said that it was emblematic of the clean sweep by the Manitobans.

When the train came to a hissing halt, the Dragoon band burst into its welcoming anthem "See The Conquering Hero Comes," a signal for the Winnipeg players, led by Captain Armytage, to leave the train. Again, there was uproarious cheering. The players, each dressed in high grey hats and the garnet colours of the club, disembarked and made their way through the huge throng, recognizing faces here and there among the jubilant supporters. Amid much bustling and boisterous celebration the players continued through the station making their way to five waiting coaches each drawn by a beautiful team of horses. Up Main Street the parade continued, giving those who could not enter the station the opportunity to shout their hosannas. At the Manitoba Hotel, there was now a more formal reception. Speeches by Mayor Jameson, club patron H.J. Macdonald and club President Nixon were given increasingly greater ovations but when

Captain Armytage said his piece, the hushed well-wishers burst into prolonged cheers and applause. Players, club personnel and newspapermen then retired to the Smoking Room, there to fill the Stanley Cup to the brim and salute one another with numerous champagne toasts.

There were other celebrations. The Vics played a benefit game on March 11, winning 5-1 over the Winnipegs. Mid-March saw yet another banquet, this time with the public invited. At the Hudson's Bay store, the Victorias' president, E.B. Nixon, arranged to have the Stanley Cup, the players' sticks, and pucks from the victory all on display. All in all, it seemed to be the warmest winter ever in Winnipeg, that year of 1896, the year Winnipeg and the West won the Stanley Cup for the first time.

128

The Cup Came Back

There's a crowd they call the Victorias and
   Montreal's their home.
They had a gorgeous silver cup and claimed
   it as their own.
But a plucky lot from Winnipeg came along
   one day
And as the Vics were off their feed, they
   stole the Cup away.
But the Cup came back, couldn't stay no
   longer
The Cup came back the very next year
The Cup came back though it was a goner
The Cup came back to stay right here.

They said: Now aren't we corkers at piling
   up a score
We're going to keep the Stanley Cup with us
   for evermore
And on our little dinky rink that measures
   eight by ten
There's nothing in the country can win that
   cup again
But the cup came back.

We fellows in the woolly west play hockey
   every day
We start to practise in July and keep it up till
   May
While down in poor old Montreal, though
   now and then they've snow,
They never know the keen delight of
   eighty-three below.
But the Cup came back.

And so the Vics got on the train and headed
   for the West
They were not saying very much but meant
   to do their best
They showed that this effete old East is very
   much alive
And played those plucky Winnipeg and beat
   them six to five.
And the Cup came back.

Source: The Globe, Toronto (4 January
1897).

The MAAA 1902 Stanley Cup Victory — A Commemoration

"Carry me true, runner of steel!
Forearm and stick be deft in the fray!
Sinew respond from shoulder to heel!
Goals, two to one, seconds to play."

The rubber is placed, the rubber is faced;
'Tis lost in the centre and shot to our end.
Their forwards are down in a scurry of brown
And back to our boundaries we flock to
defend.

It's "Block with your shoulder!" and "Check
with your hip!"
"It's Play for the corners!" and "Cover
your man!"
It's wrestle and scrimmage and scramble
and trip,
"The puck's in the open! Now! Shoot
while you can!"

They shoot: — and it flies like a crow to her
nest.
" Guard! eagle-eyed keeper, the game is
with you!"

It drops with a smack from his drum of a
chest
And drives to the side from the point of
his shoe.

A scurry, a clatter, a fall — it is mine!
Their forwards are scattered and
dazed; — in a trice
We leap through the break in their
leaguering line
And rush for their goal o'er the
snow-littered ice.

A foot from the ice, with a whir and a ring.
(Ah, joy of a moment too might for rhyme!)
It drives for the post like a swift on the wing.
But it's just too late for the whistle blows,
"Time!".

Source: Star, *Montreal (14 March 1902).*

The Goal

Thrash on the stick on the frozen sheet,
Whir of the puck as it darts away,
Crash of the shock when the rushers meet,
Skir of the skate in the snowy spray —

Oh, it isn't the thrill of a single will,
The vigour that plays like a dance of
flame —
It isn't the luck of the lofted puck
That carries the palm in the well-fought
game.

It's training of muscle and eye and nerve
In seven to play with a single soul;
It's sinking of self in the will to serve, —
It's shoulder to shoulder that makes the
goal.

Source: Star, *Montreal (14 March 1902).*

Our Seniors Victorious

On an east-bound hurrying train,
Soon our boys will be again,
Seven Victorias much alive,
For the Stanley Cup will strive.
With what anxious hearts will wait,
For the tidings of their fate,
In them we have trust, profound,
For their play is good and sound,
Scientific, strong and sure,
Stiffest hockey they'll endure,
Everyone is in good trim,
Everyone's going down to win.
Sportsmanlike — well I should think so!
Gentlemen — a toast we'll drink too.
When they play, they play like men,
There is nothing mean 'bout them,
So with hope will wait and see,
If victorious they will be.
If that much contested prize,
Cynosure of hockey eyes.
Once again a trip will take,
In our town its home to make.
"Valeran Whitney's" still in goal,
Jealously guards space, 'tween each pole.
With eyes, hands, stick, knees he risk
Nothing to keep out that disc.

Three cheers for "Whitney",
pluckey(?) old man,
Best of goal-keepers, since hockey began.
"Roddy Flett" is playing again,
He's one of their biggest men.
Biggest, best, a solid wall,
Whoso runs 'gainst him must fall,
Cleverly he plus his stick,
Takes puck out of melee quick,
Lifts it far, with coolest air,
Of all point players, he's the player.
"Charlie Johnston's" still alive,
And on hockey, seems to thrive.
Who can skate as fast as he?
Who can play so brilliantly?
Good boy. Charlie play away,
And will win the cup some day.
"Captain Dan's" still in the field,
With what force his stick will wield,
When occasion it demandeth,
Take heed ye, who think ye standeth.
When you run 'gainst Captain Dan,
You'll think you've fallen, my young man.
Then there's "Tony," and there's "Tote,"
Two good men, (or I'm no poet),
"Tony plays with dash and vim,

Very few can equal him."
"Tote" more quietly carves his way,
Just the kind to win the day.
On the forward line this time,
Is, a new man, bound to shine,
So-called "Roxy," just for short,
Clever playing is his forte.
At the last game here I'll mention
That his timely intervention,
Saved my beauty (?) from the harm,
(Here I'll tender "Thank-yous warm"),
Which that horrid, flying disc
Seemed to think I ran a risk.
There are spare men, two in number,
On the ice they never slumber:
"Magnus Flett" is cool and strong,

He'll be perfect before long,
Then there's "Sol," who plays with speed,
No one can his puck exceed.
So dear boys, our seven best,
For the glory of The West,"
We all hope you'll win the game,
If you don't, you're not to blame.
And When you're coming home,
That you will not come alone.
That the far-famed Cup Stanley,
Once again, our eyes will see.

Tommy

Source: Manitoba Morning Free Press,
Winnipeg (8 February 1900), p.5.

Faceoff

Face to face
they lean
at centre ice,
sticks poised,
bodies cocked,

eyes lowered,
concentrating
on the puck
that isn't there
but will be.

Silence, then
a sudden jerk,
Stick flash,
connect, a shot —
they're off.

Source: ZZZap Hockey (*Markham,*
Ontario: Fitzhenry and Whiteside).

When the Bay Freezes

Sometimes on hard-crusted winter snow
I've seen the game escape its limits,
And leap the width and breadth of things,
become a mad chase going nowhere, out
past dangerous places where the current
nibbles cheese holes — out to the wide
*   wide bay;*
where iceboats leave their tracks to race
*   with birds,*

and fishing shanties are lost castles beyond
*   the town,*
and snow clouds loom ahead like giant
*   goalies.*

Al Purdy

Source: Collected Poems (*Toronto:*
McLelland and Stewart).

Winter Sketch

At night the neighbourhood rink
Becomes a compartment of motion
With the twinkle and slash of skates
And the whack of wood on hard rubber.

Source: ZZZap Hockey *(Markham,*
Ontario: Fitzhenry and Whiteside).

Prospecting the Dawson City Way

The city of Dawson is about as far away from Ottawa as any city in Canada. So you can imagine the surprise which greeted the trustees of the Stanley Cup back in 1904 when they received a request from the Yukon to challenge for the much sought-after trophy. After all, the only stories one heard about the Territory were of hardships suffered by the thousands who trekked through the wilderness and cold, looking for gold and instant fortune. Sure enough there was plenty of ice around, but hockey players? . . . good enough to win the Stanley Cup? . . . well, they thought so in Dawson. But that was only natural; the place was inhabited by a bunch of hunch players who loved to play the long shot.

The first hurdle was passed when the trustees agreed to Dawson's challenge as presented by Joe Boyle. A native of Woodstock, Ontario, and a noted athlete himself, Boyle had moved west to Vancouver as a sports promoter, mainly of boxing, before deciding that there were more opportunities to make his fortune in the Klondike. Boyle was right. Soon he was active in mining, developing hydraulic methods, staking claims, making representations to governments and generally earning his title: King of the Klondike. It was while Boyle was in Ottawa negotiating with the government that he was successful in convincing the Cup's trustees that Dawson city could indeed give a good account of itself against the Stanley Cup holders. It was the greatest news since the gold-rush had led to the creation of the city of Dawson. The best-of-three series between Dawson's own and the famed Ottawa team would be played in Ottawa on Friday, January 13, Monday, January 16 and Wednesday, the 18th.

Tentative preparations in Dawson now accelerated with the news. Not even the ten thousand dollars needed for the trip was looked upon as an insurmountable obstacle. The plan was to pay the money from a post-series tour, exhibiting what they did best — play hockey.

Boyle had sent explicit instructions: all use of liquor and tobacco was to stop; a drill captain was to be selected and a daily allocation of work for each player was suggested; a diary was to be kept with all that transpired including any need for discipline, the journal to be given to Boyle upon arrival in the capital city; a conditioning program was suggested, its instructions to be strictly followed since the Ottawa rink measured 7.5 metres longer than the Klondikers'! In addition, light training apparatus, clubs and dumb-bells, walking and skating were recommended to offset the long voyage. Boyle also wanted to be sure that the series would be won by the team playing the best hockey, and to that end he convinced the Ottawa officials that no options should exist in any of the penalties: deliberate fouls would result in game expulsions. Boyle was serious about his team's chances. Sure, it would be a long shot but it would be a lot like prospecting for gold. With a lot of hard work and constant effort, pay-dirt could be struck. As far as Joe Boyle was concerned, he wanted a guarantee from each player that he would be in the best of condition and play his best.

Suitably informed, the All Klondike team made its final selections after a number of tournaments. Albert Forrest, a seventeen-year-old, would be in goal, Hec Smith would play centre, George "Sure-Shot" Kennedy at right wing, Norm Watt at left with R.N. Johnston at point, Randy McLennan at cover-point and Lorne Hannay at right point. Martin and Young were also selected. The latter was unable to leave in time for the Stanley Cup series but early enough for the Maritime tour to follow.

The great majority of Dawson players were government workers and what with an election on December 16, arrangements for travel could not be finalized until after that date. On Monday, December 19, however, it was time to move out. After all, the first game was in Ottawa on January 13, less than four weeks off — and Ottawa was more than six thousand kilometres away.

The first leg was from Dawson to Whitehorse, some six hundred kilometres distant. It was looked upon as an opportunity for conditioning. Smith, Martin and Kennedy decided to make the trip by dog-sled; McLennan, Watt, Forrest and Johnston chose bicycles. Each group was hopeful of covering eighty kilometres per day over the hard-packed snow. The distance per day didn't seem to bother the players since in their role as government officials they were accustomed to covering eighty kilometres per day in a variety of ways, seeking protection and shelter in the various sheds built along the way for such purposes. However, the weather refused to co-operate. Shortly after the players left Dawson, a thaw of sorts developed. The dog-sled was more of a nuisance than a help and soon it was abandoned at an outpost. The bicycles, not having firm ground, soon broke down and were similarly abandoned. There was only one thing to do — walk the entire distance.

Carrying all of their equipment and bags, the Klondikers were sustained only by the thought that their legs and level of conditioning would be much stronger as a result of all of this, but it was difficult. Again, the weather changed soon after they began their trek. Their feet became swollen with frost-bite. Christmas was spent in a shed still some eighty kilometres from Whitehorse. It was difficult to be cheery and optimistic with their feet swollen and blistered but the thought of being close to their first destination urged them on. On December 26, the seven straggled into Whitehorse. Albert Forrest, the young goalie, carried his boots; his feet were in too much pain from the unrelenting cold snap.

Their spirits were now high. They appeared to be just in time to catch the train which would take them to Skagway the Gateway to the Pacific. Once again though, they were at the mercy of the weather. Snow slides had occurred in the White Pass, seventeen in all, too many to clear off immediately. The Yukon railway and the team were delayed for two days in Whitehorse. Even though it seemed to be an opportunity to do some skating, again, there were problems. The rink measured twelve by fifteen metres, hardly big enough to do much in the way of serious practise. Then too, those who could get their skates on over their puffed-up feet found that there was so much sand on the ice surface that the skates were dulled beyond use.

Meanwhile, back in Dawson, reports of the team were circulating. The Yukon *World* reported that the "tramp was one long picnic for them . . . arriving at Whitehorse as hard as nails, seven days after leaving Dawson and ready for a swim each morning in the icy Skagway river in order to keep their bodies in Spartan condition." The paper added that while that type of "training is a bit strenuous for the average man, the Yukoners thrived on it."

On December 28, the train was finally able to leave for Skagway. Once more, however, misfortune struck. From Skagway, the plan called for a steamer to Vancouver followed by the train to Ottawa. The cold weather refused to relax its grip. Temperatures plummeted to -48°C. The steamboat was unable to put into the Skagway harbour. For three days the players searched anxiously to see if there was any let-up in the cold, at least enough to allow them to leave.

Finally, on the last day of December, the *S.S. Dolphin* was able to steam for Vancouver. It was anything but a relaxing voyage. McLennan wrote home to say that the voyage was extremely rough. Some tried to skip rope and exercise with dumb-bells but on the whole "all cared less whether the ship sunk or not." The ship rolled . . . and pitched . . . the heavy waves raised it high . . . and then dropped it suddenly. There was fog everywhere, making it impossible to foretell when any sudden lurches would occur. The voyage took some thirteen hours longer than expected, a delay which was further compounded when the team could not put into Vancouver. It was too foggy. On to Victoria. Again the fog would not allow the *Dolphin* to port. The captain had to make a decision. Rather than circle or drop anchor until the fog lifted, it was decided to move south to Seattle in the United States. Once there, the team hurriedly made arrangements to take the train north to Vancouver.

It was January 5 when the Klondike team arrived in that west-coast Canadian city. Word of the quest and their round-about travel had preceded them. A huge crowd, complete with civic dignitaries, was on hand to meet and greet these northern cousins. A thunderous ovation rocked the station platform; the Vancouver papers remarked, "the boys look husky and weather-beaten and say that they are as hard as nails." While the Dawson team obviously enjoyed the attention, time was at a premium. There was a train that afternoon for Winnipeg. It was important that they be on it.

The Klondikers delayed their departure until the very last moment waiting for the captain, Weldy Young, to meet them. Unable to leave with the rest, he had hoped to meet up with the team in Vancouver. When he did not show up, there was no alternative but to leave a ticket for the missing player and head for Ottawa.

Joe Boyle's original plans called for the team to stay over in Winnipeg for at least one night in order to do some skating, but the delays had scuttled that. Instead, the players continued to skip rope and exercise in the 2.5 metre-square smoking-room aboard the train. Two spares were also due to meet the team along the way: Lorne Hannay in Winnipeg and Fairburn in Rat Portage. Word of the Yukoners being aboard soon filtered throughout the train and as the trip east continued, the curious and admiring came out at each stop to wish them the best of everything. The news of their quest, as well as their arduous voyage, already becoming a legend, was preceding them. It seemed as if the westerners wanted to see the Ottawas put in their place. The *Winnipeg Free Press*

reported: "the progress of their efforts to win the greatest hockey trophy in Canada will be watched with interest as the great distance they have come and the hardship of a 450-mile trip over sub-arctic trails on foot cannot but fail to win the sympathy of all lovers of the sport." The first game was scheduled for the 13th, four days and almost sixteen hundred kilometres away. The club decided to request a postponement, secretary Watt lamenting, "the boys are in poor shape . . . we have practically no chance to keep in condition and when we get to Ottawa, will be in no shape to play."

The Dawson All Klondike team arrived in Ottawa on Thursday, January 11, only to find out that their request for the delay had been denied. The first game would still be January 13. There would be time for one practice.

In the Yukon, the newspapers were upset at the Ottawa club's rejection of what seemed to be an eminently justified request. It only went to show, the paper said, "that they, evidently, are afraid of the Yukoners because they are allowing the visitors only one day in which to practise for the match." The *Daily News* stated, somewhat bitterly, "should it (the Cup) once be landed here, it is doubtful some say that enough talent could be massed in one city to wrest it from the Yukoners." The newspaper went on to assure its readers: "Joe Boyle will see that they (the players) commit no foolishness but that they saw wood."

Friday the 13th finally came. Ottawa was abuzz with excitement. Parliament was in session; many visitors were in the city. A huge crowd was expected at the game and all in all, the Yukon received one of its best advertisements. The largest crowd ever to witness a Stanley Cup game to that point, twenty-five hundred, was shoehorned into Dey's Arena to see the plucky Klondikers who made this unimaginable trip to Ottawa, and that for only one reason, to win the Stanley Cup. The Ottawas, or the Silver Sevens as they were better known, were considered to be one of the finest teams ever assembled. For sure, they were the home-town favourites but the Golden Seven Dawson boys had clearly caught the imagination of the crowd.

Led by their seventeen-year-old goalie, Albert Forrest, the Dawson All Klondike team took to the ice for the pre-game

Klondike hockey team and manager Joe Boyle at Dey's Rink, January 1905.

141

warm-up. A roar of approval, almost admiration, greeted them, filling the cold building. After Forrest came Johnson, the point, Hannay, cover-point, McLennan, rover, Smith at centre, left-winger Kennedy, right-winger Watt, and substitute Archie Martin. Weldy Young had still not arrived. The identification of the Dawson team with the gold-rush was hard to miss. They were resplendent in their new uniforms: black sweaters with gold trim around the neck and wrists over white pants with black stockings. They were thoroughly up-to-date. Some even had the popular hollow Winnipeg's skates with thin blades. It's doubtful whether there was ever more noise in the venerable old building. It continued loud and long in anticipation of the eagerly awaited match. Even Governor General Earl Grey was in attendance. Having first been called upon to make the ceremonial face-off, he did so and retired to his seat to watch the game with his wife, the Countess Grey.

However, the excitement of the game did not live up to the anticipation. When it was over, the score was 9-2 in favour of the Ottawa team. According to *The Ottawa Citizen*: "Forrest in goal is a marvel and made some sensational stops. His cleverness and strong defence prevented a much larger score." It had been a rough game, a vintage Silver Seven exhibition of rough, tough hockey. For the first twenty minutes, the game was close, the score even. But gradually Ottawa, by virtue of its superior talent and conditioning, pulled away to lead at the end of the first half by 3-1. In the second half they outplayed the

game, but tired, Klondikers 6-1 to win by a 9-2 score.

The northerners were undaunted. Joe Boyle telegraphed the Dawson *Daily News* to keep the home-town hopes high.

The score is no criterion of it (the game) nor of the relative merits of the two teams. It was a fast rough game and Ottawa in the first half made three goals from offside plays which referee Styles of Cornwall was not fast enough with his eyes or skates to follow. Ottawa was continually offside thus putting our boys to the disadvantage which always belongs to the side playing a clean game when large liberties are allowed the other side.

Others, however, weren't as sure. *The Montreal Star* sympathized with the fatigued Klondikers but refused to consider it as an excuse having any bearing on the results. "Dawson's team was clearly outclassed," it reported. The Halifax *Herald* was blunt in its assessment: "Ottawa outskated, outgenerated and outpointed them in every department of the game . . . the second and undoubtedly the deciding game will be played Monday night."

The *Herald* was right. On Monday, January 16, before another capacity crowd, many of whom had come hoping that the series would be tied, the Silver Sevens retained their Stanley Cup with a convincing 23-2 victory. The champions were led by one-eyed Frank McGee who scored a record high, fourteen goals in the game, eight of them consecutively. The Dawson dream of a Stanley Cup victory had been shattered. As far as their supporters were concerned, the reason lay in the unsportsmanlike decision of the Silver Sevens in not allowing the travellers sufficient time to rest up from their tiring journey.

But at least the visitors had had their chance even though they would always wonder what the result would have been had they been able to rest up and have a few tune-up practices. In any event they were not ready to return home. After a reception for both teams and a week's rest, they embarked on a playing tour of the Maritimes, Quebec and parts of the United States and western Canada. It lasted three and one-half months and consisted of twenty-three games, including the two Stanley Cup games with Ottawa. Overall, the Klondikers won twelve, lost ten and tied one. On March 21, the team played its last game, defeating Brandon with a 9-1 score. Plans to continue with games in Regina, Calgary, Rossland and Nelson were abandoned because of the arrival of warm weather and the melting natural-ice surfaces.

On April 14, 1905, Albert Forrest was the first to arrive in Dawson. The youngster had finished the trip from Whitehorse to Dawson on foot after his bike had broken down. One day later, Watt and McLennan arrived by dog-sled, mushing through the mud and snow along the Whitehorse-to-Dawson route. The others, scattered along the trail, straggled into the city the next afternoon. To each, the Dawson city public expressed their praises for one of the most memorable feats in Canadian sporting history.

Erlebnis

Bumpy backyard ice,
* the scrape of blade, thrill of glide and*
* shuddering stop;*
twilight of snowy silence, echoing boom,
* clattering stick, muted shout.*
Boylike, I dreamt of heroes.
Mirrory arena ice,
* the dig of thrust, surging strode and*
* winging turn;*
nights of noisy crowds, cracking shots,
* slapping sticks, ringing cry yells.*
Youthlike, I felt glory.

Silvery mountain snow,
* the swish of powder, bite of edge and*
* spraying stop;*
days of sparkling stillness, weightless turns,
headlong schuss,
* breathless cry.*
Manlike, I knew obscenity.

W.J. L'Heureux.

144

Howie Morenz Is No More

The streets of Stratford, Ontario, seemed especially cold and damp that 9th day of March, 1937. Outside the windows of the *Beacon-Herald*, it appeared as if every citizen in town had come by to personally read the news. It was true. Howie Morenz was dead. A heavy pall hung over the town — a sombre silence of shock and disbelief. Howie Morenz, the Stratford Streak, the Mitchell Meteor, the Canadian Comet, the Swift Swiss . . . a host of memories flooded back to the adoring public, now grieving, but totally enamoured with the fastest of the Flying Frenchmen.

Memories. Howie Morenz was born in Mitchell, Ontario, on September 21, 1902, the youngest in a family of six. His parents were of German descent and chose to settle in an area with many of their countrymen. Like most Canadian boys, Howie learned to play hockey. He wanted to be a goal-tender but after a game in which twenty-two goals were scored against him, he decided to try a forward position. When he was fourteen, his family moved to Stratford where he decided to try out for the midget team. Dressed only in short pants and skates, stick in hand, Morenz was embarrassed. Not only that, he was bruised; the older, better-equipped boys took turns bumping and roughing up the newcomer. Howie was dejected. Half-way through practice, he left the ice for the dressing-room. Between sobs, he tearfully told the manager, Father Bill Gerby: "I'm not coming out any more, Mr. Gerby," while bruised and blood-stained hands were wiping away the tears.

A few days later, the Stratford team lost badly to its rivals from Kitchener. Someone remembered the youngster from Mitchell. Morenz was asked to come out again. In the return match with Kitchener, Morenz was everywhere. He became the talk of Stratford and the league.

Wherever he went, Morenz was the centre of attention. He could never get enough hockey. In one week, he played for three different teams, twelve games in eleven days, over three thousand kilometres of train travel. The opposition all appeared to be skating backwards as the young *phenom* blurred by. His parents, who had visions of their youngster becoming a musician, decided with resignation to discontinue the piano lessons their son had taken for so long. It was obvious that he would be an artist of a different sort.

Memories. There was some amusement when it was recalled that Howie was mistakenly registered as a girl with the Ontario Hockey Association. The error was eventually found but for years "Miss" Morenz took some good-natured teasing. Perhaps because of that, Howie was continually trying to demonstrate his strength. He ignored pain and continued to play with broken toes, and knees sometimes swollen as big as a stove-pipe hat. On one occasion, a car door had been slammed on his fingers; one was almost severed. The doctor set and splinted it. An hour before normal arrival time, Morenz went to the arena, had his finger dressed and put on his gloves so his coach wouldn't notice. That night, Morenz scored four goals and four assists for his awestruck Stratford team.

Soon the Stratford Streak was much sought-after. Lou Marsh, sports editor of *The Toronto Star,* as well as an OHA referee, contacted the Montreal Canadiens and Toronto St. Pats of the fledgeling National Hockey League. The year was 1923. Professional hockey was still a dirty word and looked down on by the public and the amateur leagues. St. Pats moved first, offering the youngster one thousand dollars to play the remaining five games of the season. Leo Dandurand, of the Canadiens was not to be outdone, offering Morenz a contract of twenty-five hundred, for the twenty-four-game 1923/24 season. Morenz was confused by all of the attention. After all,

he had stopped off in Toronto after a game to watch the St. Pats and the Ottawa Senators. He was in awe. Never had he seen so many skilled players on the ice at one time, doing what appeared to be the most difficult of manoeuvres with the utmost of ease. Upon returning home, he told his mother: "You don't have to worry about me becoming a professional. Those fellows are too good."

But others had other ideas. Having watched Howie score nine goals for a CNR shop team in Mount Royal, and having seen the reaction of the French Canadian fans to this will-o'-the-wisp, Leo Dandurand was even more determined to sign Howie. He sent a representative, Cecil Hart, to Stratford to sign the twenty-year-old. When Hart offered to pay an overdue tailor's bill for forty-five dollars as well as a three-hundred-dollar signing bonus, which would pay off a variety of other debts owed by the family on top of the twenty-five-hundred-dollar contract, Howie signed.

Oh, the wailing in Stratford when Morenz committed himself to the Canadiens! Many residents, thinking only of their town's hockey fortunes, felt betrayed. And for a variety of reasons: first that he would not be available for Stratford's team, secondly, that he was *turning professional,* and thirdly that he did not sign with an English team. Indeed a minister from one of the local churches railed against the Montreal team "for luring an under-age boy to the wicked city of Montreal."

The controversy continued into the summer. Finally, a confused Howie Morenz wrote to Leo Dandurand on August 10, 1923:

Dear Sir:
I am enclosing check and contract to play with your club. Owing to several reasons, of which family and work are the most important to consider, I find it impossible to leave Stratford. I am sorry if I caused any inconvenience and trust that you will accept the returned contract in a sportsmanlike way.

Yours truly,
Howie Morenz

Memories. When autumn of 1923 came, a young but more mature Howie having changed his mind again, boarded the train for Grimbsy, home of the Canadiens training camp. He was determined to gain a spot vowing to "make it or I'll quit the team." And make it he did. From the time the coach Cecil Hart teamed Morenz at centre with Aurel Joliat and Billy Boucher, he was the talk of the training camp. Morenz was stopping, starting, darting, rounding the net, gaining speed with every stride, passing, checking, shooting, scoring. Dandurand knew that he had a find but he knew the public well enough to know that the horrors of the Great War were still fresh in people's minds. It wouldn't do to have a German playing in front of French and English audiences. After all, hadn't the name Berlin been changed to Kitchener for that very reason? Dandurand decided that Morenz would be born of parents from near Zürich, Switzerland. Lightening

Legs, or the Swift Swiss would take his place among the likes of Joliat, Vezina, Mantha and the rest of the Flying Frenchmen.

Images. Morenz taking the puck behind his net, bouncing on his skates as he turns up the ice, gathering speed, the crowd rising as one in anticipation; Morenz sweeping around on through the defencemen, launching a quick shot at the bewildered goalie. The west end of the Montreal Forum belonged to Howie. Every move he made was cheered nay, exalted. These were hard-working people who knew and anticipated their hockey. They might have been down to their last dollar or down in their luck, but were rich in their appreciation of the game and its artists. They were the self-styled Millionaires' Section with its rallying cry *Les Canadiens sont là.*

Images. Even to his team-mate, the great Aurel Joliat, Morenz was scintillating:

Morenz left us all behind in a rush with the puck down to the Chicago defence where he was checked hard, the puck shooting off and getting picked up by a Chicago forward who veered into the centre face-off spot. I switched over from left wing and poke checked the puck away from the Chicago forward taking off in the same sweeping motion for the Chicago end. I had only two strides when I heard Joliat screamed at me from right wing. Even with the play going at full speed, Morenz had roared through the vacated wing, circled behind me and was now streaking like a scared cat down right wing.

To catch him before he reached the blue line, I had to fire a shot rather than pass at a stick and without losing any speed. He was through the Chicago defence in on Chuck Rayner and rifled the puck into a corner of the net before any of us fully knew what was happening.

Images. New York fans would remember their first sight of Howie Morenz for many years. The Hamilton Tiger franchise moved to New York city in 1925/26 and became the Americans. Their first game in Madison Square Garden was with the Canadiens. Seventeen thousand spectators, many seeing their first game of hockey, were mesmerized by the speedy number 7 who seemed to be everywhere at once. For the NHL, New York was the gateway to the American public and Howie Morenz was a key unlocking the door.

That same year, Morenz became even more of a hero to the French-speaking Montrealers and was more and more accepted, grudgingly, by the English-speaking fans. For while Quebec was a French-speaking island in an English-speaking Canadian sea, Montreal continued to be an English bastion surrounded by the French. The NHL was quick to see the possibilities. During the 1925/26 season a new franchise, the Maroons, was begun in Montreal as a means of attracting a following among the English and of feeding on the natural rivalry with the Flying Frenchmen. Games with *les Canadiens* were full of emotion, tension and inspired play. Morenz and his team-mates were the torch bearers in their followers' continual struggle for their own identity.

Memories. Morenz was a high-flyer off the ice as well as on. Some would say that he had a soft heart, that he could easily be taken-in with a sad story. Others remarked that Howie always remembered his poor days and hoped that his good fortunes would help make others happy. Some said that he never worried, while others were convinced that he was spending his money as fast as he was making it, thinking that he would live forever, never thinking that a rainy day would ever come. He seemed like the typical small-town boy who couldn't believe that he was in the big time and treated every day as another bonus.

He bet and lost fourteen hundred dollars at the races before his wedding day. Without hesitation, he simply went down to the Canadiens' offices and arranged for an advance on his next year's contract. On another occasion, after betting two hundred dollars on a long shot, that came second, he tore his ticket in half and threw it away. The same day, hearing that the winning horse had been disqualified, he rushed back by taxi and, after climbing the race-track fence, found the pieces with the help of his flashlight, put the ticket together, cashed it and joyfully tipped the taxi-driver fifty dollars.

Memories. In retrospect, it appeared that 1926 was the year when the public's romance with Howie Morenz fully blossomed, some of it due to his team-mate, Georges Vezina. On March 24, 1926, one week after the Stanley

Howie Morenz, the Stratford Streak.

Cup play-offs, Vezina, the popular goalie, died from tuberculosis. He had played gallantly while suffering with much pain but making no excuses nor attempting to give any less than his all. A shocked Montreal public came to appreciate the efforts of Vezina and, by association, all of his team-mates. It was a time when radio was bringing les Canadiens into many more homes. The dashing exploits of Morenz and the rest of the habitants evoked visions of fierce pride. When the depths of the Depression struck in the early '30s, Morenz represented a beacon of hope especially to his Millionaires' Section perched high above the Forum ice. Morenz was their Babe Ruth their David against Goliath, the personification of their struggle against the odds.

Memories. As with all athletes, age started to catch up with Howie Morenz. It was gradual, a little thing done with less verve and panache. People were likely to overlook the odd mistake, but they were coming more often now. By the 1933/34 season, at a time when people were in need of heroes, when they wanted even more to be carried off from their daily doldrums, Morenz's play deteriorated. For the first time in his career, Morenz heard home-town boos directed at him. It was a shock. Tears streamed from his eyes in the dressing-room; he sobbed like a child. Perhaps as much for his own good as not, Morenz was traded to the Chicago Black Hawks who looked to him to save their struggling franchise. He could not adjust. The next season, Morenz was traded to the New York Rangers. When the 1935/36 season was over, Morenz was convinced that his days in the National League were over. In Montreal, however, Cecil Hart became the coach, one of his conditions being that he would coach only if "Howie Morenz were brought back to the Canadiens where he belonged."

Morenz was rejuvenated. Reunited with Joliat and Gagnon, he was like the Morenz of old. Once again, the singing and cheering came from the Millionaires' Section. Howie Morenz was born again!

Memories. On January 28, the Canadiens were at home playing the Black Hawks. They were the Canadiens of old, leading 4-1. Morenz was in vintage form. He picked up the puck from his own end and swooped over the Chicago line, the Forum crowd rising in anticipation. Sports writer Baz O'Meara painted a word-picture:

> Then came a simple check back of the net. Disaster rode the boards as Howie went down. Earl Sibert crowded him and when Howie fell, his skate nicked into the wood and held. When Sibert fell on him, he tried to work his foot free. He rolled over. His face twisted in pain. He failed to rise. Like a game thoroughbred, he merely leaned on the shoulders of Gagnon and Joliat. Their faces, eloquent of disaster, were set in tragic lines. For them, it may have been the last time they were together and there was something gentle in the manner in which they helped him to the exit.

In the hospital, O'Meara continued, "Howie was weeping . . . not tears of pain, but tears that stronger men know when something hits them unexpectedly just when all the world is bright and gay."

Memories. The broken leg was a crushing blow to Morenz. Friends and those who wanted to be his friends, came in a steady stream to St. Luke's hospital. He was morose. Bottles were brought in an attempt to cheer him up. All the excitement, his agitated state, the constant stream of well-wishers caused him to be keyed up. Sedatives were prescribed to help him sleep at night. His weight dropped from a playing 165 to an estimated 100 pounds. His five-foot-eight-inch frame seemed to be only a mass of bones. Then, at 11:30, March 8, 1937, Howie Morenz collapsed and died. The official cause was listed as heart failure but a young reporter with the Stratford*Beacon-Herald*, Milt Dunnel, wrote, "whenever puck men gather in the steam and sweated dressing-rooms, in rink corridors, or hotel lobby, it was heart-break that caused the death of Howie."

So many memories, so many people privileged to see Howie Morenz play hockey. And now, so many more would want to pay their respects.

In Stratford, on March 10, four thousand of Howie's former fellow citizens went to the arena to pay their homage to their home-town hero. Prior to a game between the Stratford Midgets and St. Michael's College, both teams stood, hushed and in reverence, at their respective blue lines. A former team-mate of Morenz from his midget days, Walter Kelterbourne, placed a wreath over two crossed sticks at centre ice. A collection was taken in order to purchase and send a blanket of red and white roses, Stratford's colours, to Montreal. Later the road leading to the arena would be renamed Morenz Street in his honour. In the lobby of the arena was placed a large picture of Morenz for all to see. In Mitchell, Morenz's birthplace, the park where he learned to skate was named after him; as well, a cairn was erected for all to read about Mitchell's favourite son.

In Montreal, an incredulous public and his disbelieving team-mates made preparations to honour this man who had become a legend. To a great many of the Depression era, life had been full of disappointments. Sport was one of the few celebrations of life and Morenz was the most celebrated of the celebrants. His body had been laid out at centre ice of the Forum, the public invited to come and pay its last respects. Morenz's team-mates, along with players from the Maroons and the Toronto Maple Leafs, formed the guard of honour.

It was a scene befitting a tribute to a great hero. Thousands of admirers waited in long queues to pay their last respects. All morning long on the 11th of March, young and old filed silently past the coffin. *The Globe and Mail*'s Tommy Munns provided a description:

> *It was a typical hockey crowd in appearance but far from that in spirit that again taxed the capacity of the Forum. Oftimes there had been standing-room only when Howie*

played and today as his body lay in state in the centre of the ice over which he had once streaked with skates that flashed like silver, the people filled every seat and crowded the same old standing-room sections. Outside the building, thousands milled towards the entrances, unable to gain admittance, yet lingering there, a subdued quiet-spoken mob paying as best it might, its last respects to a man whose athletic ability and personality had combined to make him a great national, nay, international figure.
Strains of an organ rose over muffled coughing as the time for the service commenced. In mid-arena stood the casket containing all that remained of the personification of vitality. Flowers in almost unbelievable profusion banked the coffin and stretched to almost either side of the boards.

Well over two hundred thousand people lined the streets of sub-zero Montreal as the funeral procession made its way to Mount Royal Cemetery. The cortège seemed even slower than normal as if being held back by the thoughts of those who once again wanted to see this man whose death would signal the end of an era. Yet memories lingered. When it was time to select the best hockey player of the first half of the twentieth century, the one chosen was the Meteor from Mitchell who had shone so brightly for so many, for too short a time: Howie Morenz.

Memories.

Monsieur Joliat

Boston she have good hockey team;
  Dose Senators ees nice.
But Les Canadiens ees bes'
  Dat ever skate de ice.

Morenz he go lak' one beeg storm;
  Syl Manth's strong and fat.
Dere all ver' good, but none ees quite
  So good as Joliat.

I know heem well; he ees ma frien'
  I doan know heem himsel';
But I know man dat know a man
  Who know heem very well.

Enfant! Dat Joliat ees full
  Of hevery kind of treek.
He talk heem hockey all de day
  And sleep heem wit hees stick.

He's small but he ees bothersome
  Lak' ceender in de eye.
Maroons all yell: Go get som' 'Flit'
  And keel dat leetle fly.

Garcon! he's slippery; oui, oui —
  Lak' leetle piece of soap.

I tink nex' time I watch dat boy
  I use a telescope.

He's good on poke-heem-check, he is:
  He's better on attack.
He run against beeg Conacher
  And trow heem on hees back.

He weegle jus' lak' fish-worm do
  Wen eet ees on a hook;
An' wen he pass de beeg defence
  Dey have one seely look.

He weigh one hondred feefty pound.
  Eef he were seex feet tall
He'd score one hundred goal so queek
  Dere'd be no game at all.

Wen I am tire of travais-trot
  I put on coat of coon
And got to see Canadiens
  Mak' mince-meat of Maroon.

When Joliat skate out I yell
  Unteel I have a pain.
I trow my hat up in de air
  And shout, "Hurrah," again.

"Shut-up, Pea Soup," an Englishman
    Sarcastic say to me;
So I turn round to heem and yell:
    "Shut up you Cup of Tea."

Dat was a ver' exciting game:
    De score eet was a tie;
An' den dat leetle Joliat
    Get hanger eem hees eye.

He tak' de puck at odder goal
    An skat heem down so fas'
De rest of players seem asleep
    As he was going pas'.

He was so queek he mak' dem look
    Jus' lak' a lot of clown.
An' wen he shoot de wind from her
    eet knock de hompire down.

Dat was de winning goal, hurrah;
    De game she come to end.
I yell: "Bravo for Joliat;
    You hear: he ees ma friend."

De Henglishman he says: "Pardon,"
    An' he tak' off hees hat:
"De Breetish Hempire steel ees safe
    Wen men can shoot lak' dat."

An' den he say, "Bravo," as hard
    As Henglishman can whoop:
"I tink to-night I'll change from tea
    To bally ole pea-soup."

Wilson MacDonald

Source: New Horizons (Toronto: McClelland and Stewart).

Hail the Conquering Heroes

Whoever said that "Pride goeth before...a fall" must have had the Team Canada-Soviet hockey series of 1972 in mind. Undoubtedly, it was the most discussed and followed sporting event ever to occur in Canadian history. And while the result turned out to be in Canada's favour, it was far from the walkover it was supposed to be.

Hockey has always been close to the Canadian public; to many, it is the National Game, a Canadian specific exported around the world. There was a time when almost any team from Canada could play another country's best and win. Scores of 33-0 were common, as were world titles. Indeed until 1956, every Olympic hockey championship had been won by Canada save for 1936 when a team from Great Britain, using expatriate Canadians, was awarded the gold medal.

But the Europeans learned quickly. In 1954, the Soviet Union, entering the world hockey championship for the first time, stunned the Canadian representatives by a 7-2 score. It didn't matter that the team representing Canada was an intermediate aggregation. The Soviets had defeated a team wearing Canada on its sweaters, and could call themselves world champions. In those days of the cold war when propaganda campaigns were being bitterly waged for people's minds, there were angry recriminations being felt and expressed throughout the country. A measure of some revenge was gained the following year when the Allen Cup champion Penticton Vs won back the title by virtue of a 5-0 victory over the U.S.S.R. The Penticton team was a group of reinstated professionals, players who at one time were considered good enough to play for pay, who might still be earning some money from their hockey but not enough to make a living from it. They were simply reinstated as amateurs for purposes of the championships. Everyone in Canada was aware that, while their skill level was a cut above the previous representatives, they were certainly far from being Canada's best. The top players were playing in the National Hockey League and were ineligible for these World Amateur Hockey Championships. When the Soviet Union won the 1956 Olympic gold, it became obvious that world hockey had overtaken the type of hockey played by the amateurs in the Canadian senior leagues. By 1961, with the victory at the Worlds by the Trail Smoke

Eaters, Canada's representative team comprised of reinstated professionals, it was even more apparent that a higher level of skill was necessary if the Canadians were to maintain their world supremacy.

As a result, the mid-1960s saw an attempt at finding a solution short of sending Canada's best. That would have been the logical thing to do but, since the best were playing in the NHL and four of the six teams were in American cities, business profits, from a schedule arranged to maximize them, took precedence. The sending of an NHL aggregation was always said to be unworkable. Other solutions had to be found. One such was the formation of a national amateur team, attracting some of the best players available with educational possibilities. It was the brain-child of Father David Bauer who was put in charge of the project. Almost immediately it ran into conflict with the National Hockey League. With an expansion about to take place, doubling the number of its teams, the NHL was fearful of losing some of the better players available to the new concept. It torpedoed the move. Thus denied many good prospects needed, the national team floundered. In 1969 when a commitment by the International Ice Hockey Federation, allowing Canada the use of nine professionals for the world championships in Winnipeg, was rescinded, Canada withdrew not only from the tournament but also from any and every international competition until it could send its best.

Though Winnipeggers were bitterly disappointed at the reality of losing a tournament they had worked so hard for, Canadians everywhere seemed to applaud the decision. They were tired of seeing their representatives continually defeated in World and Olympic play, something they were convinced would not happen if they could send their best.

And so, for two years, international hockey from pee-wee to pro continued without a Canadian representative. Once again, Canadians from coast to coast focussed in on the National Hockey League's expanded version, still smug in their conviction that the World Amateur Championships were an inferior brand of our game, that the NHL was the best in the world. A writer's reflections neatly summed up the feelings:

> *There probably is not a television program in the world which has as high or as loyal a per-capita rating of viewers as Hockey Night in Canada. There is no subject in Canadian public life which so many people can discuss knowledgeably and intensively as last night's game. Hockey fans are Canada's greatest classless mass. Hockey's folklore, myths and mystiques make up the main body of all Canadian culture. Hockey has become an affair of state, a prop of nationhood.*

It was still in the spring of 1972 when an announcement was made in Ottawa by Hockey Canada, an agency created by the federal government to restore Canada's international hockey prestige. An agreement had been reached between the Soviet Union and Canada for an eight-game series in

September. Four would be played in Canada and four in the Soviet Union. The response of Canadian fans was ecstatic. At long last their best players, the cream of the NHL cream, would be selected and show the world how hockey could be played.

Throughout the summer months, when Canadians were normally enjoying the cottage on the weekend or following their favourite baseball team, the number-one topic of conversation was hockey. In July, thirty-five players and two coaches were announced as the pool from which the final team selection would be made. At first, the public response was enthusiastic, then it became a source of uproarious questioning. It was soon apparent that only members of the NHL could be selected to play for Team Canada as it was named. Effectively barred were many others including popular and prolific scorer Bobby Hull, who had joined the fledgling World Hockey Association along with a handful of other NHLers. The national Hockey League was not about to give the rival league any exposure whatsoever. As quickly as the controversy flared up it receded into the background when it was explained that the agreement was necessary in order to get the NHL's co-operation. Somewhat ironically, the Team Canada name continued as did the countdown to the first game, too slowly for most.

If there was one thing consistent with the eager anticipation of the Canadian public, it was the feeling, of novices and experts alike, that the series would be swept eight games to

none for Canada. After all, had there ever been a better team assembled anywhere? Weren't they the best of the professionals? Weren't they playing the Soviet "amateurs"? The team included such familiar players as the Esposito brothers, Phil and Tony, and the Mahovlich duo, Frank and Peter, the GAG line (goal-a-game) of Gilbert, Ratelle and Hadfield, Yvon Cournoyer, and Brad Park. These heroes, plus a starry roster of others, each one a darling of the Canadian public, would show the world. In many ways, it would be a classic confrontation on a variety of levels — the Soviet collective approach versus the Canadian individualistic one, communism versus democracy, amateurs versus professionals. But essentially, it was their hockey versus our hockey, a chance to show the Russians, and the Canadian fan could hardly contain himself waiting for September 2 and the beginning of the Super Series, a press-agent's dream.

When finally that night in September came around, the dream soon turned into a nightmare. Greeted in anticipation, it ended in despair as 18,818 spectators, including the Prime Minister, became increasingly restive within the large confines of the Montreal Forum. Another twelve million viewers of television watched in disbelief as the Soviet Union, after falling behind early by a 2-0 score, rallied with a superb display of hockey to defeat the Canadian team by a 7-3 count.

Where Team Canada had been the darlings of the public before the game, they were now the targets of their fair-weather followers. The smooth-skating Soviets, superbly conditioned and prepared, had forced all to re-evaluate them in light of their convincing display. Canadian fans were critical; editorialists fumed: "is it too much to expect," they asked, "that $50,000 to $1,000,000-a-year hockey players should be in shape in September like the Russians?" "OH CANADA!," wailed the front-page headlines of the Montreal *Gazette*. One writer borrowed an American analogy when he remarked, "to say that we took the Russians lightly is to hear General Custer ask:' What Indians?'" No more were the Canadians called Team Canada in the media. It was more likely to be the Alan Eagleson All Stars or Team NHL or Team Ugly.

When the second game of the series was over, a 4-2 Canadian victory in Maple Leaf Gardens, there seemed to be a collective national sigh of relief. Perhaps, now, the universe was unfolding as it should. The Canadians played more aggressively and in a more determined fashion, too aggressive and determined as far as some fans were concerned, but it was a reassuring victory. When game three, played in Winnipeg, ended in a 4-4 draw, it was more and more obvious to all that the series would not be the easy romp earlier predicted. The Canadian fans felt betrayed. All of the hype and promotion had led them to believe in a heady manifestation of national pride. The public's disenchantment, growing steadily since the first game, turned into resounding boos during the fourth game in Vancouver. Again, the Soviet Union won, taking a 2-1-1 lead before returning home to Moscow for the

final four games. Canadians watching television that evening saw a bitter Phil Esposito chide the Canadian public for its lack of appreciation of the Canadian players' efforts.

When the scene shifted to Moscow some two weeks later for the fifth game, the Canadian players were in some ways relieved. Never had a sporting event generated so much interest and coverage in the nation, most of it negative and of the second-guessing variety. Many of their fans had deserted them. Partly because of the four games already played plus two exhibitions in Sweden before game five, the press, in Canada and Europe as well, seemed to be leading the criticism. One of the results was that the players were beginning to find a common goal. They were bound together by the uncaring criticism levelled at them from almost every quarter. When game five was over in Moscow, the Canadian team had once again lost. The score was 5-4 even though they had enjoyed a 4-1 lead over the Soviets at one point in the game.

Now the task seemed awesome. They had won only one game, tied one and had lost three of the five played. To win the series, it was necessary to win each one of the three remaining games. It seemed impossible. They were in a hostile environment; they did not know the language; countless millions watching the games at home had apparently given up on them; some of the thirty-five originals, four to be exact, had decided to leave Moscow and return home. They had not been playing enough, felt out of shape and wanted to rejoin their own teams in

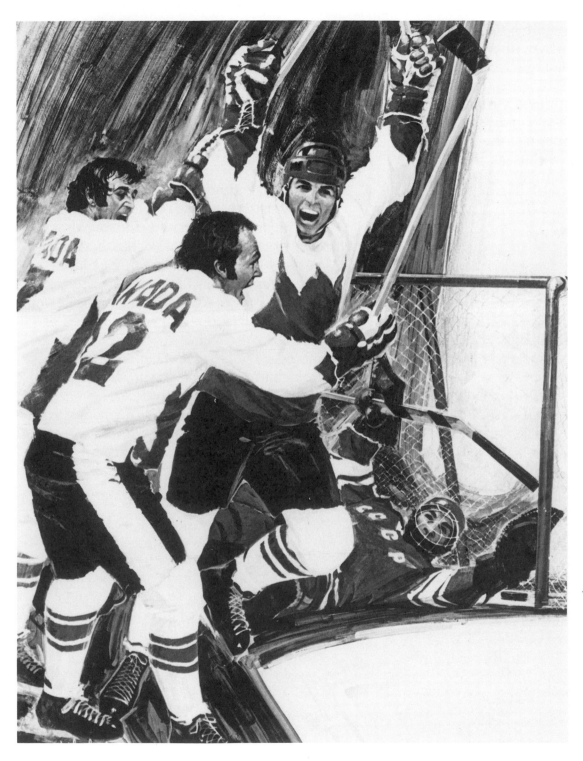

Painting **Henderson Scores** *from a photo with Cournoyer and Henderson and Tretiak. The artist included Esposito in recognition of his play during the series.*

preparation for the NHL schedule. All looked bleak indeed. About the only positive things were the belief that the players and coaches had in each other, and the very partisan and vocal three thousand Canadians who had made their way to Moscow to give their unabashed support to the now-underdog Team Canada.

Game six was played on September 24. The result, a 3-2 Canadian victory thanks to a winning goal by Paul Henderson, was greeted with restrained enthusiasm by the Canadian public. After all, two more victories were needed to win a series which was producing some of the best hockey ever witnessed. The seventh game again proved to be a one-goal victory for Canada and once more, it was Paul Henderson who scored the winning goal. The eighth and final game would decide the series.

While the hockey was indeed exciting, in many ways it seemed to be almost incidental to the great turmoil which erupted throughout the series. Ever since the selection of the team but particularly from the first game, when the Canadians not only lost but skated off the ice ignoring the international hockey practice of listening to the winning team's national anthem and the shaking of hands, Canadian fans had been constantly critical of the behaviour and sportsmanship of their team. The players, meanwhile, complained of the Soviets' more subtle illegalities; coaches railed at officials; behind the scenes bargaining was conducted with increasingly mistrusting intensity. Alan Eagleson, the chief Canadian negotiator,

seemed to be wearing too many hats: head of the players' association, NHL interests, Hockey Canada. Each day seemed to bring out a new turn in the roller-coaster of emotions. Now, all was to come down to the eighth and final game. This was the game which captured the nation's imagination and interest.

And capture them it did. The deciding game would be played at a time when Canadians were supposed to be at work or school or otherwise occupied. Yet, to look out on the streets in any city was to see and feel the quiet. In auditoriums throughout the land, giant screens were assembled and connected to video transmitters to capture the action, fittingly, in larger-than-life size. In offices, schools, stores, homes and places of work throughout the land, it seemed as if the whole country was gathered around television sets. Where television reception was impossible, radio provided the link-up. The federal election campaign continued to be ignored; Bay Street lunch hours were uncommonly long; coffee-breaks in Edmonton continued indefinitely, while in British Columbia, it seemed as if everyone was up by nine. In the Maritimes, youngsters were late in returning to school — if they returned at all. An estimated-sixteen-million Canadians, the largest viewing audience ever for a television program, shared a common experience while they gathered around their sets watching their once-again-beloved Team Canada in the eighth and deciding game of what some would later call the Summit Series.

160

It was September 28, 1972. Some eighteen thousand spectators, fifteen thousand of them Soviet supporters, were in their seats at the Luznicki Sports Arena in Moscow to witness the final confrontation. Some three thousand Canadians, their distinctive dress and flag-waving accompaniment, underlined their chants of "da, da, Canada, nyet, nyet, Soviet . . . da, da, Canada, nyet, nyet, Soviet . . . ," were beginning to make their presence felt long before the puck was dropped for the opening face-off. A cordon of Red Army personnel ringed the arena ready to curb any potential disorder.

For some time, there was the very real possibility that the final game would not take place. The Soviets had reneged on an earlier agreement, said the Canadians, that the officials for the final game would come from Sweden and Czechoslovakia. The Soviets wanted to assign the game to the West German officials, who, Canada had been assured, would not work any further games. Both sides were adamant. Embassies became involved. Eagleson and his Soviet counterpart engaged in brinkmanship. Finally, both sides agreed that each would be allowed to choose one official. When the Canadians requested the Swede, they were informed of his illness and subsequent unavailability: once again, the final game seemed to be in jeopardy. Another compromise: one official from West Germany, Kompalla, would join the Czech, Batja. Still the controversy was not finished. The opening ceremonies now presented a problem. At game four, in Vancouver, the Soviets, as their farewell gift, had made a presentation of beautiful Soviet dolls to the Canadians. The ceremony was seen live across Canada, and the Soviet Union had created much favourable publicity for itself. Now, at game eight, the Canadians wished to reciprocate with a large and elaborate totem-pole. When they were told that there was not enough time in the pre-game ceremonies to allow for such, the Canadians threatened to bring it out regardless and dump it at centre ice allowing the Soviets to explain the situation to their audience. The Canadian contingent's frustration with the whole series was by now impossible to restrain. There had been too many irritations which seemed to defy any explanation other than that they had been intentional. Prior to the game, when the Canadians had gathered for their pre-game meal, one hundred of three hundred steaks they had brought from Canada were missing. They must have brought two hundred and not three hundred, they were told.

Soon, however, all was behind them. It was time to play the game. Canada's worst fears were realized early. In the first three minutes, two interference calls were assessed to Team Canada. At 3:34, Yakushev scored to give the Soviets a 1-0 lead. When a third interference penalty was called on Canada's Jean Paul Parisé, there was a violent protest resulting in his expulsion from the game. Three thousand supporters, now greatly incensed by the turn of events, started to chant their "let's go home . . . let's go home . . ." filling the arena and travelling into the homes wherever the game was being followed. Then the Canadian bench erupted. Coach Harry Sinden threw a stool on the ice, a chair followed; Sinden was hoping to draw attention to what players, coaches and fans felt was a blatant attempt by the Soviets to steal the game. For ten minutes, the bedlam continued. The Red Army stationed themselves shoulder to shoulder around the building. In Canada, the bewildered public attempted to understand what was happening.

Finally, the game continued. Now a Russian was sent off for interference as the officials, who had called only two interference penalties in the previous seven games, called their fourth in succession in the first ten minutes of the eighth and deciding game. Canada's Phil Esposito tied the game. When another Canadian penalty was called at the twelve-minute point, the Soviet's Lutchenko restored his team's lead. The only goal of the period not scored on a power play was by Brad Park; his tally at 16:59 tied the game at 2. The close game continued into the second session. Both teams exchanged markers, as first Shadrin, only twenty-one seconds after play commenced, and Bill White, just after the ten-minute mark, put the puck behind the rival netminders, Dryden for the Canadians and Tretiak for the Soviets. But then the Canadians lapsed. Two Soviet goals by Yakushev and Vasiliev meant that they went into the dressing-room leading 5-3 after the second period. Once again the Canadians were backed up against the wall.

Team Canada's coaching staff of Harry Sinden and John Ferguson knew that they would have to score early in the third period, but at the same time, they could ill afford to gamble recklessly. A decision was made. For the first ten minutes, the team would stress containing the Soviets and hope to capitalize on an early opportunity. Only during the last ten minutes of the period would they gamble.

The third period started. Canadians put their plan into action. At 2:27, Phil Esposito converted a Peter Mahovlich pass. Now the Canadians were one goal behind. They went back to their tight-checking play. At the midway point in the period, a surprise: the Soviets, for the first time in the series, lapsed into a defensive style of play, hoping to protect their one-goal lead. Then at 12:52, Yvon Cournoyer took a pass from Esposito and slid it past Tretiak. The puck went into the net but the red light indicating a goal did not go on! Three thousand Canadian spectators and the Canadian bench were on their feet cheering. Still, the light remained off. Alan Eagleson, the Canadian architect of the series, raced to the timer's bench to protest but was immediately intercepted by a phalanx of Red Army personnel who promptly started to drag him out of the rink. This was all taking place on the side of the rink opposite the Canadian bench. Players Peter Mahovlich and Gary Bergman raced to the boards and began tugging at Eagleson's arm; the army security guards were equally insistent that Eagleson be escorted out of the premises. Soon, players who weren't dressed for the game joined in the push-pull match with the encouragement of the Canadian supporters and the astonished and stunned bewilderment of the Soviet fans. Eagleson was freed and was soon racing across the ice to the safety of the Canadians' bench, where his posse of rescuers remained. "Nyet, nyet, Soviet . . . da, da, Canada . . ." thundered the three thousand voices in unison while some fifteen thousand home-side followers, unaccustomed to seeing any authority challenged, watched, dumbfounded.

Now the game was on once again, this time with the score tied 5-5. The Soviets continued to play a defensive style secure in the knowledge that international convention stipulated that in the event of a tie in games won and lost, the series winner would be the side having scored the most goals — and the Soviets had one more than the Canadians. But the Canadians were playing with determination. The three thousand fans kept up a constant din. In Canada, it was as if all were mesmerized by the television screen or the sound of their radio. Seldom, if ever, had any nation been so totally in communion with each of its fellow citizens.

Time marched inexorably on. Five, four, three, two, one minute to play. The excitement was at a fever pitch as first the Soviets and then the Canadians took turns missing chances. Team Canada had many opportunities but the sixth goal was eluding them. With a minute to go, Sinden was attempting to put out his steadiest line of the series, Clark, Ellis and Henderson. Henderson jumped over the boards but Esposito and Cournoyer were too involved in the play to leave. Now Esposito was controlling the puck. He shot at Tretiak. The

rebound bounced out to Henderson, another shot, another save . . . but also another rebound and this time Henderson directed the puck under Tretiak's pads for the go-ahead goal. There were only thirty-four seconds remaining in the game. In the arena, the Canadian bench erupted. The players swarmed over Henderson who had scored what would be his third consecutive game-winner. Now the noise from the Canadian fans was deafening. Flags unfurled and waved back and forth. The countdown towards the end of the game was conducted with joyful bedlam. Television and radio commentators, including the venerable Foster Hewitt, could hardly contain themselves. The villains of previous games were now the conquering heroes.

In Canada, nothing like it had ever happened before. In London, Ontario, where a high-school United Appeal football game was being played at the university campus, about four thousand students listening to the game on their transistor radios broke into a resounding cheer at Henderson's goal followed by a spontaneous rendition of the national anthem at game's end. Everywhere, the celebrations spilled out. At Stratford, where *King Lear* was in progress, actor William Hutt interrupted his soliloquy, walked towards his audience, announced the score of the final game, joined in the boisterous applause, assumed his former position and picked up where he had left off. There was even the young man in St. John's, Newfoundland, who, watching the game in his low-ceilinged basement recreation room, threw his hands straight out over his head in a victory gesture with Henderson's goal and broke his fingers on the ceiling. Maple Leaf Gardens immediately began answering its phones with, "Maple Leaf Gardens, home of Paul Henderson."

Newspapers outdid themselves in their exuberance. One suggested that Phil Esposito be made prime minister; a man on the street wanted the puck to replace the maple leaf on the flag. Throughout every city and town and hamlet in Canada, thousands of citizens poured into the streets to celebrate the remarkable come-back. There was ecstatic euphoria which continued on until Team Canada returned to receptions in Montreal, Toronto, and later, Ottawa. At Toronto, some eighty thousand stood in the pouring rain for hours to hail their conquering heroes. Indeed it was the Series of the Century.

Hockey Players

What they worry about most is injuries
  broken arms and legs and
fractured skulls opening so doctors
can see such bloody beautiful things
almost not quite happening in the bone rooms
  as they happen outside —

And the referee?
  He's right there on the ice
not out of sight among the roaring blue gods
of a game played for passionate businessmen
and a nation of television agnostics
who never agree with the referee and applaud
when he falls flat on his face —

  On a breakaway
the centre man carrying the puck
his wings trailing a little
  on both sides why
I've seen the aching glory of a resurrection
  in their eyes
  if they score
but crucifixion's agony to lose
  — the game?

We sit up there in the blues
bored and sleepy and suddenly three men
break down the ice in roaring feverish speed
and
we stand up in our seats with such a rapid
pouring
of delight exploding out of self to join them
why
theirs and our orgasm is the rocket stipend
for skating thru the smoky end boards out
of sight and climbing up the appalachian
highlands
and racing breast to breast across laurentian
barrens
over hudson's diamond bay and down the
treeless tundra
where auroras are tubercular and awesome
and
stopping isn't feasible or possible or lawful
but we have to and we have to
      laugh because we must and
stop to look at self and one another but
our opponent's never geography
      or distance why
  it's men
  — just men?
And how do the players feel about it
this combination of ballet and murder?

For years a Canadian specific
To salve the anguish of inferiority
by being good at something the Americans
aren't —
And what's the essence of a game like this
which takes a ten year fragment of a man's
life replaced with love that lodges in his brain
   and takes the place of reason?
Besides the fear of injuries
is it the difficulty of ever really overtaking
a hard black rubber disc?

Is it the impatient coach who insists on
winning? Sports writers friendly but
sometimes treacherous? — And the worrying
wives wanting you to quit and your aching
body stretched on the rubbing table thinking
of money in owners' pockets that might be
in yours the butt-slapping camaraderie
 and the self indulgence of allowing yourself
to be a hero and knowing everything ends
in a pot-belly — on the ice can all these
things be forgotten
in swift and skilled delight of speed?

— roaring out the endboards out the city
streets and high up where laconic winds
whisper litanies for a fevered hockey player —
Or racing breast to breast and never stopping
over rooftops of the world and all together
sing the song of winning all together
sing the song of money all together . . .

   (and out in the suburbs
there's the six year old kid
whose reflexes were all wrong
who always fell down and hurt himself and
cried and never learned to skate
   with his friends) —

Al Purdy

Source: Fifteen Winds, A Selection of
Modern Canadian Poems (*Toronto: The
Ryerson Press, 1969*).

Grey Is The Forelock Now Of The Irishman

Grey is the forelock now of
the Irishman,
    Stickhandler of my roaring
Twenties birthright,
    F. Scott Fitzgerald of the
sporting world,
      (and, between games, father
to me).
    My beautiful brain-washed
Canadian sons
    are bringing in the whole
neighbourhood
    to see the old pro alive,
    the all-round right-wing Maple
Leaf god,
    Adonis of an era now
crumbled
    and fallen into the cannibal
maw of mobs.

The boys, crowding in at the
    door,
surround him with a fiery ring
    of worship,
envying his eyebrows,
thick with scars inflicted by

    the high sticking
of old idols, Clancy, Morenz,
    Horner —
(and, my god, one of them is
 standing at attention!)

When I was their age, unholily
    dreamful,
    full of the same power of innocence,
    I saw crowds pick him up
and carry him away,
    policemen trampled down,
    hysterical women following
their infatuation
    to the barricaded hotel-room
doors,
    crying in the corridors
    their need for illusion.

    And I remember the millionaires
who courted him
    whose money had not bought
them youth
    and the golden skates of
fame;
    one of them used to invite
him

into his suite at the Royal
York for an oyster feed,
    then ordered up by phone
    crustaceans, wine, stove,
pans, chef and all;
    another used to send him
every Christmas
     suitably engraved silver
dishes
    which my mother never
used.

I remember my father, too, in
    the headlines,
on the gum cards, in the roto-
        gravure,
and how, in the pasture, there
    was nothing
to charge but shadows and, in
    the dark beyond night,
bright enormous butterflies
    crossing the moon
of his disenchanted vision; I

heard of him cry out to them
in another room but they
    stayed in his eyes
until we were well-marked by
    the days
of his going down into ruin.

Wrinkled now is the brow of
    my all-star father
standing in the doorway
of his grandchildren generation
who must yet learn,
in smaller forums with less
    limelight,
how heroes are really made.

Joan Finnigan

Source: It Was Warm and Sunny When
We Set Out *(Toronto: The Ryerson Press,
1970).*

Shut Your Mouth Tourbin !!@*!!

We gathered
at a small table
in a far-away beverage room
to witness
a great Canadian event:
a Montreal and Toronto
hockey game.
Jon, a Montreal fan
gazed intently
at the small
coloured television set
proudly mounted
on the stage.
(In elegant fashion I might add!)
He sat, unmoved,
uttering hardly a word,
shaking his head
at every bad pass
Montreal happened to make,
slowly sipping
his glass of beer,
glancing from side to side
for some sign of security.
I wanted to tell him
that I thought Montreal
had a good team,

that they had
a good young defence
but decided not to,
any hint of inferiority
on my part
would make the night
unbearable for me.
It was bad enough
that my Toronto Maple Leafs
were in last place,
And his Canadiens,
(if you can imagine?)
in second place
only two points out of first.
We both sat motionless
for the first ten minutes
of the game,
hardly a word to each other,
slowly sipping the beer,
not taking an eye off
that television set.
"Montreal has a good
3rd period hockey team,
he said,
they're going to be
tough to beat."

"With Ferguson out,
and the way'
the Leafs are passing,"
I said,
"Montreal will be lucky
if they last till the 3rd period!"
He didn't laugh,
and even the dirty look
he directed at me
appeared as half a smile.
He knew that
I was speaking the truth,
With Toronto leading 2-1
going into the 3rd period of play
I felt quite confident.
Jon, I could see
felt very dejected.
He was searching for words
and fumbling with his beer glass.
I explained to him
that even though
his team was losing,
an honest sportsman
always commended
the good plays
of the opposing team.

He tried not
to appear disgusted
as he nodded his head
in approval,
and when I added,
"Remember Jon,
it doesn't matter
if you win or lose
it's all in how
you play the game,"
he sat up abruptly
peered directly into my eyes,
uttered a few non-syllables
and quickly poured himself
another glass of beer.
"It's easy being a good winner,"
I said,
"but it takes a better man
to be a good loser."
A stranger passing our table
asked what the score was.
I didn't say a word.
He looked at Jon.
With one quick glance at me
he shot back at the stranger
2-1 Toronto!!!!!

We didn't smile together
as the stranger
moved away from the table
for the start of the 3rd period.
Jon inched closer
to the T.V.
sitting on the edge
of his chair
carefully watching
every Montreal move,
watching Montreal move
quickly into the Toronto zone
and then with one triumphant
ALLLRIGHHHTTT!!!!!!!!
he slammed his empty glass
on the table,
stared directly at me and said,
"Montreal has a good
3rd period hockey team."
I fumbled with'
my cigarette package,
shifted uneasily
in my chair
then came back with
a very uncertain
"The game isn't over yet."

"Do you have anymore
tired clichés?" he said
as Montreal scored
their third goal
only a few seconds later.
"I haven't lost faith Jon,
like I said before,
the game isn't over yet."
He laughed his hearty laugh
then said victoriously,
"In two minutes and 42 seconds
it will be!!!"
I moved closer to the T.V.
sitting on the edge of my chair,
watching carefully
every move Toronto made.
As the waiter whisked
by our table
Jon casually ordered
another jug of beer.
The announcer could
barely be heard saying
"One minute remaining in the game."
as the crowd roared!
I stood up
as the Leafs moved

into the Montreal zone,
My eyes glued directly
on the television,
Gamble out of the net!
Leafs with six attackers!
a quick pass to Walton
Bang!!! into the top corner,
game tied 3-3
with only 23 seconds remaining!!!
I sat back
a very relieved man
watched Jon pour himself

a glass of beer
then carefully poured myself one
and Jon
without even glancing up said
"SHUT YOUR MOUTH
TOURBIN!!!??@*!!"

Dennis Tourbin

Source: Twenty Cents Magazine, London
(April 1970).

172

Standing Room Only

A player raised his hick'ry wand
    And took a might sock
to amputate, as he sailed by,
    A hated rival's block.
He smote him once with might and main,
    He smote him twice, he smote again;
And chuckled, as he laid him low,
    "The hospitals have S.R.O."

A critic sat with head bowed down
    And wrote his mournful tune:
"This constant bloodshed can't go on
    Or hockey'll perish soon.
The folks soon tire of Donegals,
    Of massacres and scream and squalls;
They'll spend their money elsewhere, so
    Take down the sign marked 'S.R.O.'"

The fan he glowered with furrowed brow
    And galloped down the rink;
Ashamed that he should be seen there,
    Down the side streets did he slink:
"I'm tired of all these clouts and hooks —
    Rough stuffs all right but wow! gadsooks!
They'll never get more of my dough
    To help the rink sell S.R.O."

The socker's team returned to town
    While press and public did their stuff
In horror that such murderers
    Should be at large — and them so rough!
And so a guy who left it late
    But figured he could crash the gate
And get a box or second row
    Just stood in line for S.R.O.

And so it goes through all the years;
    We bite our nails right to the quick
And fret and fume and shed salt tears
    And say that rough stuff makes us sick.
But when it looks as though a brawl,
    On any little feud at all,
Might come across and bring us woe,
    WE stand in line for S.R.O.

Brian Devlin

Source: Montreal Daily Star (23 February 1928).

173

Ned Hanlan — Canada's First Sporting Hero

Edward "Ned" Hanlan was a five-foot-ten-inch giant. He was such an accomplished oarsman that a favourite guessing game played by reporters was that of explaining how this one hundred and fifty-five pounder could power his shell along so quickly. In fact, one New York paper wrote that there were concealed bellows in Hanlan's boat. When pressed by his foot, this imagined ejection of jet propulsion was sufficient, it said, to puff him powerfully along. Such were Hanlan's exploits that massive amounts of publicity were generated by him. Tales of his rowing feats were so common in the 1870s and '80s that he might have been the best known of all Canadians. In fact, when a huge bronze statue of the celebrated oarsman was unveiled in 1926, long after his triumphs, the Toronto *Globe and Mail* remarked of the celebration: "The ceremony brought something of the fervour of the hectic times when any race in which Hanlan rowed was a national event of first importance, when throngs waited for hours for news of his latest feat and when the name Canada was carried around the world by his prowess."

As the son of a hotel owner on Toronto Islands, Hanlan was introduced to rowing at an early age; newspaper reports had him rowing to the mainland from his island home at age three. While others walked or rode bicycles to school, Hanlan rowed to and from the island to mainland Toronto. It was no wonder that by the time he was twenty years old, in 1875, the youngster had quite a following among rowing enthusiasts in Toronto. So much so that a group of upstanding citizens decided to form a club with the budding champion as its focal point. The purpose of the Hanlan Club was simple: look after all the details with respect to issuing and accepting challenges, and leave Hanlan only to row, exercise, eat and sleep. Not only was there prize money to win but also the gambling at the boat races was endemic. In short, there was money to be made; the Hanlan Club intended to make it.

When plans were announced in Philadelphia to hold a Centennial regatta in September, 1876, the club made the decision to enter Hanlan. Elaborate preparations were undertaken to ensure that the young Torontonian would be at his peak. Being a relative unknown in the United States would be a valuable asset to Hanlan's handlers. Ever since Americans had been victorious in every event of a Toronto regatta two years earlier, the feeling among eastern Americans was that the Canadians were lacking in top-flight scullers. If the Canadians could pull an upset they would have a major betting *coup*. To prepare Hanlan for the race, the club made arrangements to borrow the best boat available and outfit it with a major innovation — a sliding seat.

All seemed to be in order as the September regatta neared. The mechanical advantage provided by the seat contributed to excellent practice times. Club officials rubbed their hands in glee in anticipation of their expected windfall. Everything was going along smoothly — too smoothly. A major hitch developed. For some unexplained reason, Hanlan decided to sell some liquor outside of

Ned Hanlan, Canada's Boy in Blue.

his father's hotel premises. He was charged with bootlegging and a warrant was issued for his arrest. Rather than submit, thereby missing the race, Hanlan went into hiding. He always seemed to be one step ahead of the constabulary who were singularly unsuccessful in tracking down the elusive fugitive. Once, it appeared that Hanlan's luck had run out. Ned was trapped at the end of a dock surrounded by water on three sides. At the other end were the fast-approaching police, a look of obvious satisfaction on their faces. With no other alternative, Hanlan dove into the water, climbed into a row-boat and overtook a steamer loaded with picnickers and heading for Lewiston. A sputtering and disbelieving group of police watched helplessly as Hanlan, cheered on by the passengers, easily caught up to and boarded the ship.

When Hanlan returned to Toronto, he did so to a hero's welcome. News of his astounding victory was the talk of Toronto. His time of twenty-one minutes, nine and one-half seconds was a record for the three-mile course. To the citizens of a young country, it was an exhilarating demonstration of their new nationality. The twenty-one-year-old who only weeks earlier had been a fugitive from the law was welcomed back to Toronto with open arms, his previous indiscretion overlooked by the authorities. Torchlight processions and a parade through Toronto were the order of the day. It was more than a local event too. The news of Hanlan's victory was announced in Quebec where it was received with great enthusiasm.

Massive amounts of publicity were generated by Hanlan's exploits. The public seemed anxious to hear of his every move; the club was only too pleased to oblige. Whistle-stop tours were arranged prior to Hanlan's races; thousands of people were attracted to Hanlan's appearances. On occasion, Hanlan and his competitor would visit all the theatres in Toronto and Hamilton prior to a match. Before one such contest with New Yorker Fred Plaisted, an event billed as the Great Race, the two were given intense ovations, their appearance being greeted with uproarious cheering.

As an individual, Hanlan was above reproach of any kind. Descriptions of him usually included terms such as "gracious, kindly, clean, humourous, sporting and honest . . . with two sterling qualities, friendliness and cleanliness of mind." It was further stated, "the height of the ladies' ambition is to secure an introduction and all men stare in mute admiration when he is in their vicinity."

This good reputation did not always extend to the club. The Hanlan-Courtney matches probably received more publicity than any other sporting event prior to 1880. The rivalry between the two dated from the Philadelphia Centennial regatta in 1876. The Canadian won the professional competition, the American the amateur. Ever since, a dream match had been a prime topic of conversation. In 1878, the first of these three matches took place at Lachine, Quebec. Some twenty-thousand spectators lined the shore to watch Hanlan defend his title and

Ned Hanlan, World Champion Single-Sculls Rowing, 1880.

defeat Courtney in the five-mile race. The margin was small — one and one-quarter lengths — enough to create doubts in the minds of his competition, followers and gamblers. Hardly had the chauvinistic nationalism died down when the Toronto *Globe* printed the headlines: "The Great American Eagle Screeches Fraud." *The New York Times* claimed that Courtney not only threw the race, he took the one thousand dollars given him and bet it on Hanlan! The charges were never proven but they did serve to indicate that perhaps something was wrong. Another American newspaper, the *Spirit of the Times* continued to attack. Hanlan's backers were charged with all sorts of impropriety including falsely advertising a shorter race as a long one so as to bilk those who had bet on time, and sending telegrams to assistants upcourse to signal Hanlan to slow down or speed up his race.

While the controversy flourished, Hanlan made his way to England and there added the English championship to his American and Canadian titles. The steamship *Chicora* left Toronto bound for Lewiston to rendezvous with the champion. Three hundred official greeters and a brass band were aboard. As it steamed into Lewiston, Hanlan was making his way into the boarding area. The band exploded into its heroic greeting "See the Conquering Hero Comes." Having departed for Toronto, the *Chicora* met other crowded steamers. All seemed aware of the precious cargo. Passengers cheered; flags were dipped. Near Hanlan's homestead a flotilla of almost three miles in length followed. As the ship puffed into Toronto Harbour a volley of cheers rose from the mass of humanity which lined the shores. By this time Hanlan was standing on the roof above the pilot-house, seemingly held aloft by the cheering thousands, competing to be heard with the brass bands and the din of tugs, steamers, sirens and bells. Never had there been anything like it. Ashore the adulation continued: receptions, presentations, toasts, accolades followed one upon the other. A song was written about Hanlan. *The Ottawa Citizen* editorialized that he should be knighted.

In the midst of all the excitement, a rematch with Charles Courtney was announced. It was unique for a number of reasons. For the first time a commercial enterprise would sponsor a race. A Rochester, New York, firm, the Hop Bitters Manufacturing Company, would offer prize money of six thousand dollars in return for the match being known as the Hop Bitters Race. In the process, international publicity would be assured for the product. The race was scheduled for Mayville, N.Y., on Chautauqua Lake, a site which was to become the Lewiston, Maine, of rowing.

With the articles of agreement signed, the rematch was eagerly awaited. Preparations proceeded at a feverish pitch. Gamblers moved into the small town and immediately started to establish their betting odds. A grandstand for fifty thousand spectators was hastily arranged. Steamboats and river barges made preparations to follow the race, seats selling for five dollars. A special railway line was built to carry thousands of rowing enthusiasts from Canada and the U.S. into the site area. An observation train half a mile long was hired to follow the race from shore. Hotel rooms, normally selling for five dollars a week were getting twelve dollars a day. Excitement was rampant.

But the race was not to be! In what was called, by newspapers all over Europe and America, the worst sports crime ever committed, Courtney's boats were sawed in half the night before the great boat race. When Courtney refused to row in another

Unveiling a statue of Ned Hanlan, CNE 1926.

179

boat, the referee instructed Hanlan to start without his rival. The Hop Bitters man refused to pay the stakes claiming that since the race did not take place, there could be no winner. During the next few months, rumours were everywhere. Courtney's people had Hanlan drinking too much, causing his backers to request a postponement. When this was refused, they said Courtney was offered the whole purse if the match could be arranged. When these options were refused, they continued, Hanlan's people destroyed the boat. The Canadian version was that Courtney knew he was the inferior sculler and, being embarrassed to lose, sawed his boat in half. More fuel was added to the controversy when Courtney produced a letter from the Hop Bitters man promising two thousand dollars win or lose. Suspicions mounted. Then Hanlan produced a letter from Courtney offering the Canadian three thousand dollars if he allowed the American to win. There seemed no end to the uncertainties.

The public would simply not allow such an inconclusive atmosphere to last. The clamouring for a rematch was so insistent that, again, articles were signed for the third and final episode in the series. All the participants were the same for the May, 1880, race. Care had been taken to guarantee an event this time. If one of the oarsmen refused to race, a substitute, Jim Riley, was available.

The site was the Potomac river in Washington. Again intense enthusiasm surrounded the match. Upwards of fifteen hundred Canadians made their way to the American capital. On race day a crush of humanity thronged to the site of the great and long-awaited event. Streetcars groaned with the weight of passengers inside, outside and on top of their roofs. An estimated one hundred thousand spectators competed for the best-viewing areas. Businesses closed; both houses of Congress adjourned; U.S. President Hayes joined the British ambassador at the vantage point of a steamer. At six o'clock, the long-awaited match began. At the start, Hanlan quickly built up a lead and at the one-mile marker he was ahead by twelve lengths. At two and one half miles, Hanlan was so far ahead that Courtney stopped rowing, turned around and started to row back towards the starting — which was also the finishing — line. To add to the confusion, Riley, the substitute oarsman, also started rowing towards the finish. In Toronto, contradictory reports were telegraphed from the race site to the thousands who were waiting, watching and listening for information after each mile. To them it appeared that Courtney was in the lead. Hanlan, sensing what was happening, put on such a spurt that he passed both Courtney and Riley touching off a chain of celebrations within the harbour. Whistling steamboats, the cheers of thousands and floating red balloons hailed Hanlan's victory. The Boy in Blue was more popular than ever and immediately the wheels were set in motion to challenge the world champion, a six-foot-six-inch Australian by the name of Edward Trickett.

At five foot ten inches, Ned Hanlan was continually the object of speculation. How could he row so well? Was his sliding seat that much of an aid? Did the time provided by his club's management give him that much of an edge? Was his technique so polished as to ensure his championship status? Of course all were important but, as well, Hanlan had the additional tool of what was then known as gamesmanship. Today it would be referred to as psyching out an opponent. Most of Hanlan's races were over a distance of four to six miles; strategy or a race plan played an important role. Seldom did he win by great margins, but he always seemed to have a sense of pacing, a knowledge of when to make his move and carry it through. His 1880 race with Trickett is a study in gamesmanship.

Because of the obvious difference in size between the two colonials, English writers busied themselves extolling the strength of Trickett. Odds on the Australian soared as the race day approached. Meanwhile back in Toronto, a line-up of knowing Canadians, two blocks long, waited outside the Bank of Montreal's Yonge Street branch. Forty-two thousand dollars was wired to English bookies by H.P.J. Good, one of Hanlan's backers.

Racing distance was four miles, four hundred and forty yards. One hundred thousand spectators lined the serpentine, historic Thames River course. An exploding cheer accompanied the start. Roughly one-third of the way down the course, at Hammersmith Bridge, Hanlan, with a three-length lead, stopped rowing. The crowd turned quiet. Trickett picked up the pace and closed the gap. Above the course, spectators, massed on the bridge, saw Hanlan again spurt into a three-length lead. Spontaneous applause from viewers along the shore acknowledged Hanlan's power. Suddenly the Canadian rowed over towards them, gave thanks for their cheers and moved back into his lane. Trickett rowed on. Again Hanlan opened up a three-length lead. Once more, he allowed his oars to drift while Trickett strained with visible effort to pull even — only to find Hanlan had, once again, pulled ahead by three lengths. At this point, some fifteen minutes into the race, the unpredictable Canadian stopped again, this time to talk with some spectators watching the race from the vantage point of a nearby steamer. Among them was William Elliott whom Hanlan had defeated the previous year over the same course. They had not seen each other since that time and it seems that they had some catching up to do. This done, he started rowing again only to stop opposite the Bull's Head Hotel, headquarters of the Canadian contingent. A wave of his handkerchief and Hanlan was off again. Trickett was soon caught, passed, and once again, Hanlan settled into a three-length lead.

By this time the huge English crowd had been completely won over. With a fearful suddenness, however, the admiring cheers turned to astonished gasps. Hanlan collapsed! His oars dangled armless in the water. His body had slumped forward in his shell. Trickett strained to take advantage, closed the distance to two lengths, one length, even . . . . Abruptly, Hanlan sprang into action, smiled at Trickett, waved to the onlookers and pulled away once more. In the final yards of the race, he was rowing consecutive strokes first with the right oar and then with the left as the boat zigzagged to the finish line. He was world champion.

Over three continents, his prowess was widely acclaimed. Rowing experts claimed that his was the perfect style. For the next four years Hanlan was supreme in the world of rowing. Every match he rowed was of national concern to his countrymen. At a time when a young country, so soon after Confederation, was attempting to create a nation using iron and steel links, the enormity of Hanlan's accomplishments served to create living proof of what the National Dream was to make manifest.

Hanlan held his world title until 1884 but continued to row competitively until 1897. He became rowing coach at Columbia and the University of Toronto, and eventually an alderman in his native Toronto. In 1908, again his fellow citizens turned out in record numbers. This time, however, it was a hushed and silent gathering. Ned Hanlan was dead. In 1926 a grateful city unveiled a heroic bronze of Ned Hanlan at the Canadian National Exhibition grounds where it still stands today, close to the scene of so many of his triumphs. The inscription at the base reads: "Most renowned sportsman of any age, whose victorious career has no parallel in the annals of sport. Victor in three hundred consecutive races. His achievements are all the more worthy of commemoration by his display of that spirit of true sportsmanship which is held in honour in all fields of sports." Immortalized in bronze, the native son was later enshrined in verse:

No more we'll trust to fickle fame
The honour due to Hanlan's name,
The champion sculler of his time
His laurels won in every clime.
No victor with Olympic crown
Brought his country such renown;
As if propelled by magic grace
His boat was foremost in the race.
The thrilling cheer we hear anew —
Hanlan wins — The Boy in Blue —
The shout resounds from shore to shore
To hail the champion of the oar.
No more again let it be said,
"Canada forgets her glorious dead."
In sculptured bronze he'll live again
And take his place once more 'mong men.
O'er island lake lagoon and bay,
His noble spirit holds its sway.
Like some Greek god returned to earth
To mark the place that gave him birth.
By Lake Ontario's surging foam,
By his beloved island home:
But more than in the sculptor's art,
He lives in each Canadian's heart.

Source: Telegram, Toronto *(3 September 1926).*

Edward Hanlan
An Epinikian Ode

I

Hail to the champion sculler!
   Toronto's manly son,
Who, across the line, and on the Tyne,
   Hath famous victories won!
And with three cheers for Hanlan
   The champion of the oar,
Let us shout, Hurrah for Canada!
   The land which such hero bore.

II

In ancient Greece the victor,
   Who at Olympia strove,
Was crowned with wreaths of olive
   In Jove's all-hallowed grove;
His person was held sacred,
   Kings his companions were;
And envied the fate of the happy state
   Which claimed him for its heir.

III

At Pytho and at Corinth,
   The athlete's prize who won,
Shed glory on his country,
   His kindred, and his town;

His statue in the temples,
   In ivory and gold,
By the side of gods and heroes
   The gymnast's prowess told.

IV

Returning to his people
   Fresh bays the conqueror waits;
The city battered down its walls
   To make him wider gates,
And joyous crowds in triumph
   The champion bore along,
While a Pindar sang his praises
   In loftiest strains of song.

V

But no victor at Olympia,
   Nor by the Isthmian strand,
Ever received such welcome
   On reaching his own land,
As that awaits the champion
   Who ploughs the Atlantic's foam,
With impatient keel and heart right leal
   Returning to his home.

VI

Save that no worthy poet
    For him shall wreathe a lay,
Since none with equal laurels
    Such victor garland may.
He won at the Centennial,
    And by Ohio's waves,
And where the Eastern river
    Past Hampton seaward raves.

VII

Toronto, Pittsburg, Barrie,
    The city, "Quaker" hight,
And the lovely Bay of Burlington
    Bear witness of his might.
He won in every contest,
    At each regatta won,
Till at Lachine he overcame
    Columbia's foremost son.

VIII

Now, shame on the foul slander
    Of those who meanly tried,
At Courtney's cost to pander
    To a boastful people's pride;

For Courtney was defeated,
    Not for the want of will,
Nor by the bribe of treason,
    But by superior skill.

IX

From sea to sea victorious,
    He left his home a while,
To gather bays more glorious
    In Britain's sea-girt isle;
And how he played with Hawdon,
    And how sponged out his shell,
With tears of mirth and laughter,
    The Tyneside pitmen tell.

X

Last, matched with England's champion,
    On Tyne's excited tide,
To see his daily practice
    The flocked from far and wide;
Each touting wharfside ranger
    The mystic magic sought,
Which the Canadian stranger
    Had lurking in his boat:

XI

With air-bags and machinery,
　　the miners stoutly held,
Or by some secret influence,
　　His skiff must be propelled;
For never such a sculler,
　　Of form so lithe and fine,
Or such modest mien, had yet been seen
　　On the Thames, or on the Tyne.

XII

But no man knows save Hanlan,
　　If even Hanlan knows,
How fast his bark can travel
　　When at best he rows:
Like the flight of an eagle's pinions,
　　When to the sun he soars,
Is the graceful sweep and powerful stroke
　　Of his well-feathered oars.

XIII

Now, not a few such striplings
　　This broad Dominion rears;
Since Wallace Ross and Warren Smith
　　Are well nigh Hanlan's peers.

Girded with North-star vigour
　　And nurtured by the sea,
By mountain, lake and river,
　　A hardy brood they be.

XIV

West of the Rocky Mountains,
　　Such youth you may behold
Braving the Fraser's rapids,
　　In venturous quest of gold;
And where Muskoka's camp-fires
　　Cast up a ruddy glare;
Where Madawaska's springtide floods
　　Their floating forests bear;

XV

Where Montmorenci's bridal veil
　　Its shower of pearls displays;
And where thro' mountain-gorges green
　　The Metapedia strays.
These eastward turned and waited
　　Impatient for the day,
When their compatriot might win
　　Tyne's championship away.

XVI

The day has come! From midnight
 Until the dawn broke clear,
Crowds lined the banks in serried ranks
 And every wharf and pier;
With craft of all descriptions
 The river was alive;
Each bridge with human beings
 Swarmed like a great bee-hive.

XVII

The champions take their stations,
 Promptly each take his place,
In the sight of all the nations
 Of the Anglo-Saxon race.
"Now, three to one," roared Elliott,
 "That I lead all the way!"
And his stalwart arm and lusty form
 Might feebler foe dismay.

XVIII

Such challenge disregarded
 Might not unnerve the youth,
 Whose speech was on the unwon victory
Was written out, good sooth!

The boast was scarcely uttered,
 "They're off!" the umpire cried,
And away they sped, but Hanlan led
 With oars superbly plied.

XIX

Like arrow from the bowstring,
 Swiftly he sped along
Past Grindstone Quay, past Redbeugh
Bridge
 And all the astonished throng,
Past the meadow-isle, whose human tides,
 Like billows, sway and roll,
And by ten good lengths a winner,
 Swept gaily past the goal.

XX

Then from the river's crowded banks,
 From roof-top, bridge, and pier,
Thrice thirty thousand lusty throats
 Sent up a mighty cheer;
And many a British city
 Caught up the wild acclaim,
And the Western world from sea to sea
 Resounded with his fame.

XXI

And while St. Lawrence to the Gulf
*   Majestic takes his way;*
While through the Thousand Islands
*   His sunlit waters play;*
While soft auroras chase the stars
*   Athwart our Northern skies;*
While Indian summer tints the woods
*   With iridescent dyes;*

XXII

While the maidens shall weave chaplets
*   In Huron's maple dells'*
While o'er Rimouski's jewelled snows
*   Shall ring the Christmas bell;*
While great Niagara's thunder-stroke
*   Th'affrighted rocks shall shake;*
While the long moonbeams nightly play
*   Across Ontario's lake;*

XXIII

While Ottawa, from storied cliff,
*   Uplifts her crown of towers;*

While modest merit still shall charm
*   This Canada of ours;*
So long in distant story,
*   As time tolls on apace,*
Shall it be told by young and old
*   How Hanlan won the race.*

XXIV

Now three good cheers for Hanlan!
*   Our flag to the breeze unfurl'd,*
For the Champion of two continents,
*   The champion of the world!*
And three times three for Canada,
*   Land of the brave and free,*
The youngest of the nations:
*   The Home of Liberty.*

W.H.C. Kerr

Source: (Toronto: Belfords, Clarke and Co., 1879).

Jacob Gill Gaudaur

77-years young
Thursday, April 4th, 1935

A message of cheer and greeting
We're starting herewith on it's way
To one whose renown isn't fleeting
Though he's seventy-seven today.
To Jacob Gill Gaudaur extending
A Hearty and lingering cheer,
And all the good wishes we're sending
Are ardently, wholly sincere.

His name has place that's outstanding
In circles devoted to sport,
And still has a fame that's commanding
Wherever good oarsmen resort.
No need that the tale be repeated
Of records still holding their place,
Of scullers he met and defeated,
Of coolness displayed in a race.

Jim Stanbury, Rogers, O'Connor,
Ned Hanlan and Hosmer and Beach,
Are names to remember and honour,
With greatness pertaining to each.
Ed, Durnan and Teemer, and Barry,
And Trickett, and Riley and Haines;
All great among oarsmen — they carry
A measure of fame that remains.

And ranking along with the greatest,
His name overshadowed by none,
Whose course, as he steered, was the
straightest,
Like the list of his victories won,
Was Gaudaur, a master of rowing,
The man who could sit in his boat
And pulling his oars, get it going
At speed never equalled afloat.

He rowed in a great many places;
Men thrilled to his gathering game;
They eagerly followed his races
And greet each win with acclaim;
And now that his contests are finished
And days of keen conquest are o'er,
We greet him with pride undiminished,
And wish him success as of yore.

A man that Orillians admire,
Still upright, and stalwart, and strong,
His record can help and inspire
The youths who now follow along.
May this be a day to pass brightly
For him who is famous as 'Jake';
May glad years to come pass him lightly
With never a care in their wake.

Admirer!

The Race

The boats sit as one in the afternoon sun
  in their quest for a rowing gold,
For each man in the crew, the feeling runs true
  the chance for a medal to hold.
They'd give an eye tooth in that moment of truth
  to row to the victory stand,
Let pride fill their chests to have beaten the best
  and drown in the clapping of hands.

But back to the gate where the grim reaper fate
  will winnow the wheat from the chaff,
As the starter retorts, "Get those shells on
their course
  we'll start in just two and ahalf."
The oars line each side, as the waves the
boat ride
  and balance precariously so;
All muscles are tense, as the oarsmen no sense
  that there's less than a minute to go.

As they set up the boat, their hearts in their throats
  the last coxie's nodded his head,
At the half-up they're poised, each handful of boys
  while the words of the starter are said.
"Are you ready?," a blast, as the shells are shot
fast away from the starting gates green.
The rates are quite high, as the men seem to fly
  past their puddles so sharp and so clean.

The race will be tight, for there's six in the fight
  and only a deck at the quarter,
The cox yells for ten and then ten again
  but six boats respond in the water.
The bodies all sway and each seems to say
  "I'm driving with all that I've got."
The aching increases, and all thinking ceases,
  as muscles and tendons all knot,
"I'll not be the one when this race is done
  who didn't give it his best,
Just 1000 more with this leaden oar
  to sweep the boat over the crest."
You lengthen your stroke to your cox's shrill croak
  as he leans to feel the boat run;
Fast hands — controlled slide, the shell seems
to glide
  yet past the point where it's fun.

You can't seem to breathe and a sickening heave
  you feel inside starting to build,
An eternity seems to have past in between
as a blast
  your ears seem to fill.
It's over and done, the big race you've won,
  so slump in exhaustion and bile.
The picture again of mind-throbbing pain,
  and bodies stretched out in a file.

Yet soon you recover, your shell, well, you
  love her,
    you've come a long way since the spring.
And now you've won gold, and the record
I'm told,
    well done, for winning's the thing!
The other boats, too, sit looking at you;
    their chances of winning now done;
You see in their faces they'd love to trade places,
    as they row away into the sun.

It's your moment of glory, your completed story
    the wish that you'd had past years
While slumped in the stern, you watched
winners and yearned
    and swallowed to hold back the tears.
You stand forth a crew, that's not easy to do,
    but you strived and sweated to grow . . .
In a sport that takes time to mold champions
sublime,
    a challenge that few really know.

As the bow leaps ahead your body feels dead,
    you wonder how long you will last . . .
Till of to port side an opponent has died,
    your shell keeps knifing on past
No thoughts where you lie, just sweep hard
and cry,
    for you're certain that you'll have to stop.
Tears mingle with sweat as another boat yet
    seems to mirror your slides at the top.
Then drive back exploding, your power unloading
    itself through the end of your oar,
With 500 left and this long boat to heft,
    the coxswain pleads for some more.
So you dig down inside to where you store pride,
    and somehow the energy find,
To take it up quick and somehow to stick
    to that pace ingrained in your mind.

Lorne Davis

Source: Catch *(September/October 1978).*

190

How Renforth, New Brunswick, Got Its Name

If you ever travel to the Maritimes, make sure you stop by the Saint John area. More particularly, visit one of its suburbs, Renforth, situated on the beautiful Kennebecasis River. The area is one rich in rowing tradition; some of the best boat crews ever to come out of the Atlantic provinces, in fact some of the best in the world, have plied those waters. Indeed it was through the sport of rowing that the village of Renforth was first given its name, starting with events in 1867.

Confederation was an important event in Canada. The provinces of Upper and Lower Canada united with New Brunswick and Nova Scotia to form a new member among the family of nations. Yet there was a certain amount of apprehension. After all, what was a Canadian? Of what was he capable? Some of the answers were forthcoming before the end of the year.

When the news was received in Saint John that an International Exposition was to be held in Paris, France, that year, there was not much excitement generated until it was discovered that among the sporting events would be the World Amateur Rowing Championships. To the people of Saint John, rowing was then as hockey is to Canadians today. Immediately a provincial crusade was set in motion to send Saint John's top crew from the Western Rowing club. Robert Fulton, George Price, Samuel Hutton and Elijah Ross, three fishermen and a lighthouse keeper were the pride of Saint John, the talk of the town. Who could ask for better representatives at Paris? The provincial government agreed and backed up its faith with a grant of two thousand dollars. The citizens thought likewise; they contributed four thousand dollars.

So it was that the Saint John crew, with their six thousand dollars, two boats and a special guardian agent, Sheriff Harding from Saint John, left their Acadian homeland to row against the best in the world in far away Paris, France. They were the pride of the Maritimes. It was written that while that area had not sent the traditional exhibits to the World Fair, works of art, indigenous handicrafts, minerals or machines, something more was on display for all to see. An identity was taking shape. On display, wrote a newspaper of the day, was to be "an exhibit of our energy, our hardihood and pluck as shall render us famous among all the famed at that grand international tournament."

The Europeans weren't impressed. After all, the leading boat clubs from London and Paris were there, looking quite dashing in their outfits and their sleek boats. By contrast the Canadians were quite a sight. Their uniforms of flesh-coloured jerseys, black trousers held up by suspenders and their pink caps were described as quaint, while their rowing style of short strokes powered only by their arms was all wrong. The boat was home-made, described as a Chinese puzzle painted green, and outweighed the beautiful English boats by one hundred pounds. While all others rowed with a coxswain who shouted instructions and steered the boat, the Saint John crew had none, preferring to steer by means of a foot-guided rudder.

Nonetheless, when the first event was completed, the in-rigged fours, the Canadians had won such an easy victory that George Price calmly waved to the crowd as the boat crossed the finish line. In the second event, for out-rigged fours, the Saint John's four were taken more seriously but even though England's top crews of Oxford, the London Rowing Club and Leanders were entered, again the quaint Canadians won by three lengths and pulling away.

Not only had the Canadians won prize money of three thousand francs and the title of the World Amateur Champions, they had earned the admiration of all those who had witnessed the event or had read the news carried by the recently built telegraph link between the old and new world. Immediately preparations were made to welcome home the champions who would be henceforth known as the Paris Crew. All of young Canada rejoiced in their glory, these bold Maritime friends . . . now our fellow countrymen in name and in fact. At Saint John a massive outpouring of emotion took place. Carriages, wagons and horses on land, steamers, row-boats and canoes on water all waited exuberantly for their heroes. The city was gaily decorated in bunting; flags were flying; the Saint John band rang out its victory anthem: "Hail The Conquering Heroes Come." Cannons roared their salute while fireworks blazed forth and a large fire balloon made its way spectacularly skyward. It was the happiest of times, and before the night was through the Paris Crew was given the freedom of the city along with a purse of five hundred dollars each, in grateful tribute.

There was an aura of invincibility about the Paris Crew. When an upstart crew from New York, the Ward Brothers, challenged the pride of the Maritimes, having earlier defeated an inferior Saint John crew, it was of national concern. The Montreal *Daily News* wrote that they were not representing Saint John alone but rather, "British North America, including the Red River Settlements (if not Newfoundland and Prince Edward Island)." The easy victory by the Paris Crew reassured everybody.

By now the champions were in great demand. Rowing was the great Canadian sport. Thirty thousand people had turned out to see the race with the Ward Brothers, causing

Canada's first World Champions, 1867.

sharp-eyed promoters to think in terms of a major Canadian regatta. Lachine, Quebec, was chosen as the site. The Paris Crew was matched with a champion English crew from Newcastle. The race, held September 15, 1870, was billed as The Great Boat Race.

By this time the Paris Crew was rowing in a much lighter, specially constructed boat. Thousands turned out to watch the Paris Crew practise. People were still talking of the 1869 Lachine regatta when a crew from Toronto rowed against the Maritimers. The Paris Crew toyed with their opponents, getting so far ahead that they stopped at the half-way mark and shared a bottle of claret while the Upper Canadians struggled to catch up. But these were not Upper Canadians they were rowing against in 1870. These were champion oarsmen from England, from famous Newcastle, and their stroke, the equally famous James Renforth.

Race day dawned, rainy, windy and stormy. Postponement was suggested. Promoters would have none of that talk, too many out-of-towners had made the special trip to Lachine. The three o'clock starting time was delayed until 6:00 pm. There were murmurs among the crowd but the throng of thirty thousand patiently made themselves as comfortable as possible along the six-mile course.

At six o'clock the winds had subsided somewhat. The race started. Within minutes the winds increased. The water became choppy. The Paris Crew's boat, not having side walls and sitting low, began to take in water.

Renforth's Tyne Crew won but the Maritimers refused to accept the defeat. The editor of the Saint John newspaper believed it was providential intervention rather than Renforth's boat that had defeated the home-town favourites. When the results were posted outside the telegraph office in Saint John, where a large crowd was following the race via wire reports, the first reaction was disbelief. Faced with reality, however, the large gathering immediately pledged four thousand dollars for a return match to be held anywhere but at Lachine. Similar offers were made to Renforth's crew from Halifax and Springfield.

Renforth deferred. They had been away from home far too long and they were anxious to return. Gloom turned to despair among Saint John citizens when it was announced, early in 1871, that the Tyne Crew had disbanded. A rematch now seemed impossible.

As spring arrived, however, so did a new hope. Renforth wired from England that he had put together a new crew. They would be willing to race in New Brunswick in August. Immediately life began to quicken throughout the area. Everywhere talk was of the upcoming international match. People ventured their opinions about protections against choppy waters. No over-confidence about this one. Price, Hutton, Fulton and Ross would be ready this time. Terms were drawn up. The race was to be for five pounds sterling and the world championship title; the distance, six miles with a turn, the course along the Kennebacasis River starting from Torryburn Cove.

The Paris Crew from Saint John.
Top: George Price, Robert Fulton. Bottom: Elijah Ross, Samuel Hutton.

195

As far as all were concerned, the eyes of the world would be watching and newspapers urged all Saint John citizens to curb rowdiness and drinking. Regardless of the outcome, it was suggested that the Tyne Crew should have only the most pleasant memories of New Brunswick. When Renforth's crew arrived on July 28, they were met with an enthusiastic welcome; Saint John opened its arms.

Race day was August 23. Grandstands were hastily being built along the finish line. Tickets were being bought as fast as they appeared. Steamers were offering a limited number of seats aboard ships which would sail beside the course, offering an excellent vantage-point. Trains offered special excursion fares from all parts of Canada and the United States. Accommodations were booked solid. The city fathers declared August 23 a civic holiday and encouraged all to see the contest.

Gamblers moved into Saint John; soon the Tyne Crew was listed as 2-1 favourites. The inevitable rumours started, the main one being that the Tyne Crew would lose this match leading to a deciding race to be rowed in Halifax the next week. Race day couldn't

The world-famed Paris Crew of Saint John, N.B.

come fast enough for most. Everything seemed in readiness. Starting time was set for 7:00 am allowing for any number of delays. If water conditions weren't suitable to the Paris Crew they had the final decision as to when the race would begin.

By 4:00 am the morning of August 23 many spectators were in their place. Trains arrived every half-hour laden with passengers, as did steamers. All roads to the race-course were jammed with carriages, bicycles and pedestrians. By seven o'clock the anticipating thousands lined the shores of the Kennebacasis. They were described as a black mass of humanity.

Prolonged bursts of applause greeted both crews as they made their way to the starting line. Then silence was followed by a huge roar as the boats knifed their way through the waters. At the half-mile mark the Paris Crew stroking 44 per minute took a slight lead. At the three-quarter-mile mark, some six minutes into the race, the Paris Crew opened up a three-length lead. Cheers filled the valley. Suddenly the Tyne Crew veered their boat toward shore. A mixture of cheers, boos and silence followed as the Paris Crew continued to row finishing the six-mile race with a time of 39:20.

As the Canadians rowed on by themselves, thousands were asking questions: What happened? Had Renforth feigned illness when he saw that his boat would lose? For it was Renforth who had collapsed, wasn't it? Had Renforth been bribed and sold the race? Was Renforth poisoned?

At 8:45 James Renforth died. The news was like a thunderbolt. An eerie quiet descended upon Saint John; all celebrations stopped. Flags flew at half-mast. The victory previously cheered seemed insignificant.

The next day an inquest was held. The doctors said that it was probably exertion. The Tyne Crew said that they were hardly working. The crew suggested that Renforth had gone for a walk prior to the race; he might have been offered a drink and was poisoned. The third day into the inquest, it was decided to examine the contents of Renforth's stomach. With no local facilities available, the closest equipped laboratory was at Boston. Two weeks later it was announced that there was no poison found. It was October 27 when the cause of death was given as heart failure.

To the people of New Brunswick, the death of James Renforth was as if one of their own had died. Poems of tribute were written; a fund was started for his widow; the St. George Society erected a cairn at Gateshead Tyne and the little town of le Chalet changed its name to Renforth, a name it carries to this day.

The Race, and the Death of James Renforth

1. Five-and-twenty thousand people gaze upon
   the river bright;
   Steamboats, wood-boats, race-boats,
   sail-boats, all form part of one grand sight;
   Mortals rushing upward — downwards —
   eager all the race to view.
   Pink the colour for New-Brunswick, for the
   English boat, the blue!

2. "Are you ready?"shouteth loudly, Thomas
   Jones, the referee;
   "Sire, we are!" eight oarsmen answered,
   almost instantaneously;
   Eager all were for the contest, O, how eager,
   none can know,
   But the Tyne boat first got water, when the
   referee said: "Go.!"

3. See, Tyne's leads our struggling oarsmen!
   look — they're leading them no more!
   Ross and Fulton, Price and Hutton, never
   better did before;
   Eager, earnest, and ambitious — past the
   English four they fly.
   And soon fifty feet they lead them —
   pleasing each New-Brunswick eye!

4. Then it was that noble Renforth, over all the
   world renowned,
   Gathered all his strength to pass them, while
   he heard the cheers resound
   From the shore and from the people, and
   then he knew well what was said:
   "In the stern boat is James Renforth, and
   the Paris Crew's ahead!"

5. "What's the matter?" shout the masses, will
   the English try no more?
   See, the Tyne men now are hasting with
   their boat toward the shore!
   In it comes with Renforth moaning, and
   before an hour had fled,
   Five-and-twenty-thousand people, told
   about the oarsman dead!

6. On the Paris men continued, hearing louder
   cheers from shore;
   On they went, without their rivals, till at last
   their work was o'er:
   But they little knew — brave fellows, how
   the noble Renforth fell,
   — A sad victim of ambition — at the work
   he lov'd so well!

7. As they hear the dreadful story, wearers of
   both pink and blue,
   They speak of their heartfelt sorrow,
   sympathy for England's crew,
   Four brave fellows, to us strangers, weep
   o'er his cold, lifeless form;
   Shall we cheer when thus they're weeping, or
   shall true hearts to them warm?

8. It was well enough this morning, for our Paris
   Crew to cheer.
   When its strength we often doubted, and for
   each hope had a fear,
   Well enough to show we loved it, and of
   nothing sad to think,
   And to mingle with the masses, with our
   nice bouquets of pink!

9. But now cease those shouts of gladness, cease
   to shout so long and wild,
   Though we're glad that on New-Brunswick,
   victory again has smiled;
   'Tis an hour for human sorrow — sympathy
   from yours and mine,
   And our Paris oarsmen kindly tell of
   Renforth of the Tyne!

10. Who will tell the tale in England to his little
    child and wife,
    How across the broad Atlantic their
    protector lost his life?
    Lost his life whilst bravely striving for his
    country and his crew!
    Who will tell the tale in England? tell me —
    tell me — tell me who?

11. O, whoever tells the story, let him to the
    widow say:
    "Dying, he spoke of a dear one in a land
    was far away;
    But one word he could speak loudly as he
    parted with his life,
    'Twas not one about the boat-race, 'twas the
    simple word of "wife!"

12. Fame he's won, and nobly won it, but he'll
    seek it nevermore!
    All his challenges and races, all his victories
    are o'er!
    All his wild and vain ambition, has, forever,
    from him fled,
    Rivals nevermore need fear him, for he's
    numbered with the dead!

13. *Let there be no great rejoicing, though the*
    Paris Crew has won!
    For Death's proved the champion oarsman,
    and his work was quickest done!
    He has taken "o'er the river," that young
    oarsman in his prime
    And he's proved to all the nations, he can
    make the quickest time!

14. *In the streets and in the city, alleys, dwelling*
    houses, stores;
    Men are telling of the oarsman, who no
    more will need his oars;
    There are but few men who sigh not, there
    are but few eyes are dry!
    And the flags for Tyne and Paris, all are
    waving half-mast high!

Byron DeWolfe

That's Where the West Begins

A football field, a Grey Cup date, and teams from Hamilton and Winnipeg seem to be the ingredients for interesting and far-reaching developments: a controversial tackle by Lou Kusserow on Winnipeg's Tom Casey in the '53 final, Ray Bawel of Hamilton being tripped by a fan in '57, the Tiger Cats' Ralph Goldston being ejected from the '58 game, overtime in '61, fog and sixty minutes played over two days in '62 and the high winds of '65. It's doubtful, however, that any of these games had as much effect on football in Canada as the 1935 meeting between these two clubs.

The Grey Cup had been donated by Canada's Governor General in 1909 to be awarded to the champion football team in the country. There wasn't a great deal of fanfare at the time. As a matter of fact, although Canadian Champions had been declared since 1892, no team west of the Ontario border competed for the title until 1921 when the Edmonton Eskimos took the long train ride to Toronto to play against the Argonauts. The Eskimos did what team after team from the West were later to do — they lost. To a section of the country already smarting from what they considered to be eastern dominance of their affairs, the loss was not so graciously accepted. Oh, the Grey Cup game wasn't yet the national celebration it was to become in 1948, but it was national and competition between East and West was eagerly sought-after. Each loss was grudgingly accepted, the narrow ones such as Edmonton's 13-1 loss in 1922 signalling hope, the 1923 Queen's University 54-0 victory over the Regina Roughriders demoralizing.

The Depression years couldn't have been more gloomy in the West: unemployment was high; dust storms swept across the prairies; the Grey Cup stayed in the East, not in Toronto and Hamilton but places like Kingston, Ottawa, Sarnia and Montreal. Would the West ever win?

By 1935 a group of Winnipeggers decided to do something about it. Games had been played for many years between the Manitobans and teams from the neighbouring United States. In the process an elaborate scouting system was devised. Names of good prospects who might be of help to the team were filed away for future consideration. For a long time Western teams had relied upon players from the East since the game had more or less evolved there. But by the 1930s the traditional game had changed. Interference or blocking was now allowed, albeit only three yards, as was the forward pass. American influences were being felt more than traditional British ones.

When the forward pass was used in the first Grey Cup game of 1929, the practitioners were Canadian. Its second Cup use in 1931 pointed out something that Winnipeggers were quick to grasp. The Montreal team of 1931 was undefeated due to the strong and accurate passing arm of the import, Warren Stevens. It was so obvious. Americans had been brought up on interference and forward passing. Why not use Americans to win the Grey Cup for the West?

Two men named Joe played a role in Winnipeg's football fortunes. The first was Joe Louis the second Joe Ryan. Louis the boxer was christened the Brown Bomber by the press; the gold-and-blue-clad footballers became known as the Blue Bombers rather than the official Winnipeg Football Club. Ryan, the club manager, was responsible for collecting a group of players who made the Blue Bomber epithet believable. During the spring and summer of 1935 Joe Ryan went on an extended tour of the neighbouring American states, the Swede belt it was called. In his pocket was a list of prospects and seventy-four hundred dollars. When he returned he did so with commitments from seven American players. Added to the two already with the Winnipeg team, it meant that nine Americans and three Canadians would represent the Manitobans in their bid

to win the right for another try at the Grey Cup.

That summer, the nine became household names in Winnipeg: Fritzie Hanson, Bob Fritz, Bud Marquardt, Joe Perpich, Bert Oja, Herb Peschel, Nick Pagones, Russ Rebholz and Greg Kabat. In anticipation of the glories of the coming season, the week commencing September 7 was set aside as Rugby Week in Winnipeg. A parade of floats, bands and stage-coaches, displays in store windows, and a campaign to sell tickets and "boost football, boost Winnipeg, boost Manitoba" were all part of the festivities. Even the 1934 Grey Cup-champion Sarnia Imperials would be played — and in Winnipeg. When the locals handed the Easterners their first defeat in fourteen games, before a record crowd, their optimism could hardly be contained. It was the first victory ever by a Western team over an Eastern. After so many disappointments, hope again resurfaced. Could recovery from the Depression be far behind?

Winnipeg's plans seemed to be falling into place. First the Roughriders of Regina were set aside by a 13-6 score. Calgary Bronks provided the next play-off opposition and they too were eliminated, 7-0. The Western hurdles had been overcome — but many other teams had been in this situation before. There was a measured sense to the celebrations. Grey Cup day was still three weeks off and winter's windy blast had already blown into the West. To add to the uncertainty three teams in the East were still in the running, Hamilton, Sarnia and Queen's University.

Governor General Earl Grey.

203

Ryan and his associates decided that the three weeks would best be spent at Detroit, Michigan. There, the team could take advantage of the weather to practise, and they would be close enough to allow for scouting at the Eastern finals, and to see their eventual competitors, the Hamilton Tigers.

The Eastern representatives were a legendary group. They toyed with an overmatched Queen's University team while winning 44-4. Against the 1934 Grey Cup champion Sarnia Imperials, the Gashouse Boys of Hamilton trailed 3-2 but broke the game open in the third quarter *en route* to a 22-3 victory. There was no doubt about it, they were impressive. They weren't fancy, they just did everything well. Defensively they dared one to get by them. Sure-handed tacklers like Seymour Wilson and Jimmie Simpson seemed to take delight in bringing much bigger men down to the ground. Their coach and quarter-back, Johnny Ferarro, was the newest idol of the city. But perhaps the object of everybody's affections was the Old Man of the Mountain, Brian Timmis. He was a one-man wrecking crew, seemingly capable of carrying a whole team of opponents on his back as he tore through the line or sifted through his opponents to stop the ball-carrier. If all of that wasn't enough, the game was to be held in Hamilton in front of the noisiest and most enthusiastic fans in the country, a group that would be even more so because of the threat of the All-American Winnipeg Machine.

As the game day, December 7, arrived, anticipation of victory in Winnipeg and Hamilton heightened. Opposition teams were asked their opinion of the outcome, Westerners favoured the West, Easterners the East. Knowing Manitobans spoke in glowing terms of the strength of Winnipeg's line and back-field. Their line outweighed Hamilton's by fifteen pounds per man. Statements by playing coach Bob Fritz and manager Joe Ryan endeared the Blue and Gold to their public. Fritz's strategy was simple: "open up right from the kick-off, get the jump and put the onus on them." Ryan was more blunt: "The Tigers will never be able to stop our running attack." People from the 'Peg heard and they believed; in Manitoba, Winnipeg was the 3-1 favourite to win the West's first Grey Cup.

In Hamilton, there was the notion that all Westerners had lost their bearings. The Tigers were touted as the strongest team to represent the East since their powerhouse of 1929. The rules for the game were familiar to Hamilton and strange to Winnipeg. The Tigers were injury-free; they were on their home field. On top of all this, the West had never won a Grey Cup game! All of this Western talk about Winnipeg was too much for one Hamiltonian, who wrote:

> *Out where the tackling's a little weaker,*
> *Out where the aspect's a little bleaker,*
> *Out where the kicks are a whole lot shorter,*
> *Out where the player's heads are mortar,*
> *That's where the West begins.*

It was a slippery field that greeted the two teams for the opening kick. True to Fritz's

204

*The Grey Cup donated by
Governor General Earl Grey
in 1909.*

prediction, Winnipeg scored an unconverted touchdown on the second play of the game to take a 5-0 lead. Hamilton narrowed it to 5-3 at the end of the first quarter as a result of a field goal. During the second quarter, the nimble, fleet-footed, half-back Fritzie Hanson took over with his bursts up the middle and scintillating punt returns.

Winnipeg scored a converted touchdown while the Tigers could only counter with a single point from a rouge (a point scored when a kick into the end zone cannot be returned to the goal line). The half-time score was Winnipeg 12, Hamilton 4.

In Winnipeg, traffic was nowhere to be seen. It seemed that everybody was glued to a

The first Grey Cup champions from the West.

206

Fritzie Hanson, Winnipeg's premier player 1935.

radio listening and hoping for a miracle. There were no half-time ceremonies at Hamilton's Amateur Athletic Association grounds. A short rest and the two teams were back to start the second half.

Nothing is as dangerous as a cornered Tiger and that's the way Hamilton played in the third quarter. Bob Fritz fumbled; a Tiger picked it up only to be brought down by a high tackle from Winnipeg's Bert Oja. High tackles were illegal and Oja was sent from the field forcing Winnipeg to play one-man short with eleven men. Hamilton scored; the score was now 12-9. Now the momentum seemed to be with the East. Turville punted for the rouge. Winnipeg was ahead 12-10. Winnipeg was forced to punt. Hamilton again drove down field, was stopped and punted deep into Winnipeg territory. The tide appeared to be turning in favour of the East. Winnipeg needed a big play to regain control.

Now the Hamilton tacklers were racing down the field to their quarry. Fritzie Hanson, the transplanted North Dakotan, waited anxiously for the ball to catch up to him. The punt return had been Winnipeg's best play in the first half gaining a total of 182 yards. It was the phase of Winnipeg's game that Hamilton players knew they had to control to win. Now Hanson had the bounding ball, he eluded a hurtling tackle and headed upfield. Hamilton players angled to cut him off. Hanson slowed down and cut to the inside as a host of yellow and black shirts skittered by. Hanson now turned upfield, saw an opening and with a knowing burst of speed accelerated to the goal-line seventy-five yards

away. The cheering was loudest in Winnipeg as the West converted and took an 18-12 lead into the fourth quarter.

Each time Hamilton moved down field in the final fifteen minutes, expecting to pin Winnipeg in their own end with their superior punting, Hanson came to the rescue with his returns. Only a safety touch was added by the Easterners; Hanson added a further ninety yards in punt returns giving Winnipeg a total yardage of three hundred and sixty-seven (in those days blocking was not allowed on punt returns). The Grey Cup moved West for the first time on the galloping heels of Fritzie Hanson. The 18-12 victory was a signal for celebrations.

The game was barely over when Winnipeggers poured out of their homes and into the streets. Gone were cares about the Depression, unemployment and railway problems. Winnipeg and the West had won the Grey Cup. Portage Avenue in downtown Winnipeg was a mass of happy exuberance. Upwards of three hundred telegrams were received by the Grey Cup champions within minutes of the victory. Immediately, preparations were made to welcome home the conquering heroes.

In the East, the Tigers were subdued and gave full credit to the new champions. To many, however, the victory signalled the beginning of wholesale recruiting of American players to the detriment of the development of Canadians. The Winnipeg team of 1935 provided a model for others to follow in search of the Grey Cup, and the lesson was not lost on many.

In the West, however, and in Winnipeg in particular, there was no thought to such serious consequences. It was a time for celebration. Their boys had won the Grey Cup. Thousands prepared to meet the newest objects of their affection. As the train neared the Manitoban capital, three planes were sent in formation to fly the twenty miles with the train from Dugald to Winnipeg. It was not yet nine in the morning when the train pulled into the station to be met by a rousing reception. Businesses had closed; a holiday spirit prevailed as the motorcade made its way through the streets of Winnipeg. The players were introduced to a rising crescendo of cheers, the loudest of which were saved for Fritzie Hanson, Winnipeg's newest idol. To place everything in the proper perspective, the *Winnipeg Free Press* published the following tribute:

> *Out where the flashing Hanson dashes,*
> *Out where Ed James and Kabat crashes,*
> *Out where Bob Fritz directs the play,*
> *Out where Oja knocks them the other way,*
> *Out where the Grey Cup is come to stay,*
> *That's where the West begins.*

Source: Winnipeg Free Press *(9 December 1935).*

Timmis' Exploits

This Timmis gent is a grizzly bear,
When he leads the Tigers from their lair.
Just try to stop him if you dare!
The Old Man of the Mountain.

With his big, right fist, and his glittering eyes,
He outplayed guys like you and I,
And he still can hit that line on high,
The Old Man of the Mountain.

In sixty-seven years, or more,
When the Tigers needed a major score,
The Tiger fans will rise and roar,
The Old Man of the Mountain.

And he'll tuck his beard inside his sash,
And hand some foe a friendly bash,
And hit the line for a ten-yard dash,
The grand Old Man of the Mountain.

Ted Reeve

Source: Telegram, Toronto *(22 October 1934).*

Brian Timmis, immortalized by Ted Reeve as the Old Man of the Mountain.

Ted Reeve as a member of the
Balmy Beach club.

212

Grey Cup Fever

The Westerners in Stetsons had just bounded
    off the train,
They yelled, "It's Grey Cup Fever and we got
    it once again!"
They seized some local yokels and they cried,
    "What is the score?"
"Are the Tigers any better or will the
    Bombers win once more?"
The locals shrugged their shoulders and said
    "Gents, that's up to you . . ."
"We are off to Narrangansett to pursue a
    steed or two."

They fell into a bistro and their merry
    leader said:
"Now tell us true, bartender, pal, what is the
    scoring spread?"
"Is it Ti-cats by a TD . . . or six-five and
    take your choice?"

And the barman looked up puzzled at this
    most unseemly noise:
"All I know," he answered quietly . . . with
    his face suffused in pain . . .
"Is that good old Charlie Dressen signed with
    Dodgers once again."

Slightly irked the strangers rumbled down
    the leading thoroughfare
As they whooped, "We're here for the Grey
Cup . . . and we're loaded up for bear. . . "
They stopped a group of students with a
shout . . . "You boys in blue . . .
"Do you like the Winnipegger or prefer the
Bengal crew?"
The eldest student answered . . . in his
throat there was a lump
"Mahovlich ain't scoring and the Leafs are
    in a slump."

So all the midweek mornings these puzzled
    Western fans
Roamed here and there in Hogtown with the
    questions in their hands
One bird sold them a soccer pool . . . and
    then some luncheon dames
Cut them in upon a raffle for some figure
    skating games.
And when at last the lads encountered some
    Toronto folks to show

A wave of gridiron interest they received the
    final blow
They were going with Cookie Gilchrist to the
    game in Buffalo.

Sour Grapes McGruffey

Source: Ted Reeve, "Grey Cup Fever,"
Telegram, *Toronto (28 November 1962).*

Frank Cosentino was a quarter-back in the Canadian Football League, his ten years being divided among Hamilton (seven years, five Grey Cup appearances, two wins), Edmonton (two years), and Toronto (one year).

He was head football coach at the University of Western Ontario when they appeared in, and won, two Vanier Cup championships in 1971 and 1974.

He has a BA in Honours Business Administration from Western, a BPE from McMaster, and an MA and PhD from the University of Alberta. Currently, he teaches Sport History at York University where he is a Professor in the Department of Physical Education, Recreation and Athletics.

He is married with four children. He and his wife Sheila live in Toronto and have a summer home in Eganville, Ontario.

Frank Cosentino has authored or co-authored eight books on Canadian sporting history, his most recent being *The Renfrew Millionaires: Valley Boys of Winter 1910.*